Co

*For all at Causeway Comprehensive School
and especially for the students 1989-1992.
Whatever is of use in this book
was brought out by them.*

We can make our minds so like still water
that beings gather about us that they may see,
it may be, their own images,
and so live for a moment with a clearer, perhaps even a fiercer life
because of our quiet.
W. B. *Yeats*, The Celtic Twilight

Faith is the beginning and love the end;
and the union of the two is God.
Ignatius of Antioch

Introduction

There are so many books on the market on prayer and on ways of praying that adding another to the pile might seem questionable. Despite all that's available, however, it's often difficult to find something suitable for someone just beginning to pray or for someone who wants to renew their prayer.

There are lots of schools of thought, lots of different ways of praying and lots of books which map these out. This book tries to offer something very basic – a flavour of different ways and approaches, different stepping stones for someone trying a few faltering steps. It will hopefully lead its users to move on, to want to learn more, to move into what's already around.

In putting it together I am drawing on some of the experiences I've had in teaching young people and in giving talks and retreats.

The most important thing about prayer is deciding to pray and sticking with that decision. It's a journey, a pilgrimage, a setting-out. To pray is to make the supreme act of hope and confidence. To pray is to dare to believe, to light a candle rather than to curse the darkness. It is an act of faith in oneself and one's own dignity and uniqueness in the sight of God. To pray is to take a huge risk. Who knows where it may lead or how it may change us? Life is lived in greyness, there is very little that is black or white. To pray is to introduce a source, a fire, a light that warms and invites and reaches into the shadows.

The where of praying is important and so too is the when. Once you have decided to pray, deciding *when* is vital. It doesn't always have to be at the same time or in the same place but having continuity is also important. Many people like to pray at the beginning and at the end of the day, others like to create a special time during the day. Making it prayer-time is what is important, a special time for you and for God. This in itself is a prayer – an option for creating a source of life and growth and strength.

Our God is a God who waits, who longs for us to open our hearts and lives to him. Our God is the God revealed to us in Jesus, who shows us the road and who walks the road with us. Deciding to pray is deciding to enter into relationship. To be a Christian is to follow Christ, it is a choice for relationship. This is a two-way thing of course, a journey and a time of waiting, a time of surprise and wonder. It is a time of discovery. Above all, we discover in praying a God who can often seem hidden and distant but who ultimately reveals himself as a God who loves. As St John tells us, God loved us first; this makes all things possible.

If I learned anything about prayer it is because my parents first taught me to pray. Out of all they have given me it has been the most precious gift.

CHAPTER 1

Morning Prayer

Whether you tumble out of bed and embrace the day or whether you drag yourself out inch by inch with dark mutterings, to begin the day with prayer has long been a part of Christian life. Praise, thanksgiving, meditation and petition have always been basic. These form the basis of the suggestions here.

We begin our day:
In the name of the Father, and of the Son and of the Holy Spirit.

No matter how the day seems it is a new day. No matter what lies ahead, there is hope. Hopefully there is also reason to give thanks and praise.
Glory be to the Father and to the Son and to the Holy Spirit.
As it was in the beginning, is now and ever shall be,
world without end. Amen.

The Psalms are among the oldest prayers and poetry we have. They span a whole range of emotions and experiences. You might now take one of those given here or take one from the section on the psalms further on.

Psalm 8
How great is your name, O Lord our God,
through all the earth!

Your majesty is praised above the heaven;
on the lips of children and of babes
you have found praise to foil your enemy,
to silence the foe and the rebel.

When I see the heavens, the work of your hands,
the moon and the stars which you have arranged,
what is man that you should keep him in mind,
mortal man that you care for him?

Yet you have made him little less than a god;
with glory and honour you crowned him,
gave him power over the works of your hand,
put all things under his feet.

All of them, sheep and cattle,
yes, even the savage beasts,
birds of the air, and fish
that make their way through the waters.

How great is your name, O Lord our God,
through all the earth!

Psalm 62
O God, you are my God, for you I long;
for you my soul is thirsting.
My body pines for you
like a dry, weary land without water.
So I gaze on you in the sanctuary
to see your strength and your glory.

For your love is better than life,
my lips will speak your praise.
So I will bless you all my life,
in your name I will lift up my hands.
My soul shall be filled as with a banquet,
my mouth shall praise you with joy.

On my bed I remember you.
On you I muse through the night
for you have been my help;
in the shadow of your wings I rejoice.
My soul clings to you;
your right hand holds me fast.

Now give some time to silent meditation. Whether you just become quiet, by using the ways suggested in other sections, or whether you use a passage or a line of scripture, is not important. Just make this time special, between you and God; and make it a time that brings you peace and life for the day ahead. If you wish to use a scripture passage, you might find the following ones helpful or you could go to chapter 14 for a Gospel piece or to chapter 15 for other passages. Sometimes it helps to stay with the same passage or phrase for a few days or even longer. Coming back again and again to a bible passage can help to uncover its riches. So much depends on our mood or needs at a particular time. Passages speak to us in different ways at different times.

1. Romans 12:9-13

Let love be genuine; hate what is evil, hold fast to what is good; love one another with brotherly affection; outdo one another in showing honour. Never flag in zeal, be aglow with the Spirit, serve the Lord. Rejoice in your hope, be patient in tribulation, be constant in prayer. Contribute to the needs of the saints, practice hospitality.

2. Isaiah 58:9-11

If you take away from the midst of you the yoke, the pointing of the finger, and speaking wickedness, if you pour yourself out for the hungry and satisfy the desire of the afflicted, then shall your light rise in the darkness and your gloom be as the noonday. And the Lord will guide you continually, and satisfy your desire with good things, and make your bones strong; and you shall be like a watered garden, like a spring of water, whose waters fail not.

3. Isaiah 61:1-3

The Spirit of the Lord God is upon me, because the Lord has anointed me to bring good tidings to the afflicted; he has sent me to bind up the brokenhearted, to proclaim liberty to the captives, and the opening of the prison to those who are bound; to proclaim the year of the Lord's favour, and the day of vengeance of our God; to comfort all who mourn in Zion - to give them a garland instead of ashes, the oil of gladness instead of mourning, the mantle of praise instead of a faint spirit;

4. Micah 6:8

And what does the Lord require of you but to do justice, and to love kindness, and to walk humbly with your God?

Now spend a few moments placing any needs you have before the Lord. Pray also for others and for the Church and the whole human family.

The Our Father is the prayer of Jesus. It is the pattern of all prayer. It is the invitation to see God as a loving and caring Father. We pray it so often that it can tend to become a rushed and uninvolved thing. Maybe at this time of the day you could pray it slowly, praying each line and allowing it to be a really sincere prayer.

Our Father who art in heaven,
Hallowed be thy name.
Thy kingdom come. Thy will be done
On earth as it is in heaven.
Give us this day our daily bread,
and forgive us our trespasses
as we forgive those who trespass against us,
and lead us not into temptation,
but deliver us from evil.

St Teresa of Avila, a great mystic of the Late Middle Ages, once wrote:

Christ has no body now on earth but yours,
no hands but yours,
no feet but yours.
Yours are the eyes through which his compassion looks out on the world;
yours are the feet with which he can go about doing good;
yours are the hands with which he can bless.

Are there ways today in which you could be this presence of Christ to others? Think of some practical ways. The following prayer is based on this and is a good one with which to finish this Morning Prayer and to launch out into the day:

Lord Jesus, I give you my hands to do your work.
I give you my feet to go your way.
I give you my eyes to see as you do.
I give you my tongue to speak your words.
I give you my mind that you may think in me.
I give you my spirit that you may pray in me.
Above all I give you my heart that you may love in me
your Father and all humankind.
I give you my whole self that you may grow in me,
so that it is you, Lord Jesus,
who live and work and pray in me.

In the name of the Father, and of the Son and of the Holy Spirit.
Amen.

CHAPTER 2

Praying in Silence and Meditation

Life can be full of noise, of hustle and bustle. Sometimes we feel strange if there is silence so we fill the silence with words or we turn on the television or the radio or whatever. When faced with silence we fidget and get uncomfortable and try to end it.

Yet silence can give us so much! Have you ever tried to listen to what you can hear when it's really quiet – the background sounds, even the sound of your own breathing? In the heart-to-heart world of prayer, silence is so important. There can often be no need for words or you might just need very few. What can we tell God in prayer that he doesn't know already? Sometimes we need to say things in prayer, but sometimes what we need to say is part of the busy world we have left in order to pray. We really need to let go of this busy world. Coming to quiet can have a deepening effect, bringing us away from all the things that bother us on the surface of our lives and putting us in touch with the essential.

Listening, waiting, watching: these are all powerful images and experiences in the Bible and in Christian spirituality. 'Wait for the Lord, his day is near.' 'Stay here and keep watch with me.' God invites us to wait with him, to come to quiet with him. God speaks to us in a thousand ways that often have nothing to do with words. In one way it's wasting time. In another way, it's the most important time we can give ourselves.

The image of the fountain can help. A fountain can have many levels or tiers. Each level is designed to be filled with the water gushing out of the fountain. To do this, it must be empty of rubbish or anything that might clog it up. When each level is filled, it then allows the water to flow out into the next level. Those who allow themselves to be filled with silence, and the peace it can bring, are first filled themselves and then let that peace flow out of them. They are cleansed of all the rubbish, the things that clog up life and cause blockages.

An old man was once asked how he prayed. He replied, 'Sometimes I sits and I talks to God and sometimes I just sits.' He had something precious. St Paul speaks of 'the things that no eye has seen and no ear has heard, things beyond the mind of man, all that God has prepared for those who love him.' For the life to come we wait; in this life God waits for us to come to peace in him.

In praying in this way, to use a cross or a candle or an icon can be of help. Starting with some music, or using the music of nature in the sea or trees or a stream, or the peace of a mountain can lead us into silence.

In this form of praying we come to allow the famous prayer of another great mystic, Julian of Norwich, to reveal its truth to us:

All shall be well
and all things shall be well
and all manner of things shall be well.

Peace be with you. Do not be afraid.

Much has been made of using Eastern techniques in this form of prayer and some people get quite excited about this, in the belief that somehow all this influence of the East will end up brainwashing people or will empty prayer of its Christian core. This may be a valid concern in some cases but, as long as we remember that it is Christ who is at the heart of the silence, and that coming to quiet is really only tuning our hearts to beat with his heart, we need not worry.

Coming to Silence
First of all find a place to become quiet. It can be a special corner of your room or a favourite place in the church or in the garden. Use a candle or a cross or icon if you wish. Sit near them and keep your eyes fixed on them. You could also close your eyes if you

wish. Sit comfortably, feet on the ground if you are on a chair or bench, hands resting on your lap. Try to sit as straight as you can. You may decide to start with ten minutes or so and can add to this over time. Now begin to become quiet, allow your breathing to deepen and listen.

Listen for all the sounds around you, starting with the sounds outside the room or building or in the distance. Become aware of them, sift through them, identify them. They don't have to be a distraction; they don't have to upset your prayer. Bring them with you.

Now become aware of the sounds near you, in the room or church, in the area around you. Listen to them too, the noise of a fridge or clock, the sound of someone walking through the church, the sound of water or birds singing. All of these sing in harmony with creation. Bring them with you too.

Finally, become aware of your own breathing and of yourself. Become aware of the growing peace and stillness. Stay with the quietness if you can. Open that stillness to God. Let his peace fill the silence. Let all that clutters your life fall away. Let all that burdens you be held outstretched before you. Let all that gives you life and joy sit there too. There is no need for words. Let whatever is in your heart speak for itself. This is all that is needed, just to sit there in silence, waiting for the One who comes.

At times you may take a word or phrase to repeat over and over again. This will put you in touch with something basic and of power and it will deepen your silence. Stay with it no matter what distractions come. Even if the whole time of prayer seems like a series of distractions and wanderings, don't worry. There are no rules for success, no targets, no qualifying points to be reached. It is the heart which communicates and this time of silence will have its own effect on your life and on your day. Even the very giving of this time is a prayer and an act of faith, hope and love.

I offer the following words and phrases that you might like to use. Choose one or find your own.

Come Lord Jesus
(or 'Maranatha' in Aramaic, the language of Jesus).

Come Holy Spirit.

Jesus is Lord.

My Lord and My God.

Peace be with you. Don't be afraid. It is I.

Jesus.

Be still and know that I am God.

I am the light of the World.

Blessed are the poor in spirit.

If anyone is thirsty, let him/her come to me.

Who do you say that I am?

You are the Christ.

Other resources
There are many other exercises and ways of coming to silence. There are ways too of moving on and allowing ourselves to be carried by various meditation exercises that will put us in touch with God in a whole range of ways.

One of the best people to learn from here is Anthony de Mello and I suggest you use some of his writings. You could begin with *Wellsprings* (Image, New York 1986) or *Sadhana: A Way to God* (Gujarat Sahitya Prakash, India, 1983).

Conclusion
Don't expect miracles, blinding flashes of light, strange music or instant heavenly peace! The silence has a power however. Perhaps its greatest strength is that it allows us to come to quiet, to get rid of all the baggage and to open ourselves to God. There are no guaranteed ways. God always remains beyond anything we can imagine or experience. Our faith and hope and love can only bring us part of the way. In the stillness can be the dancing however; only in the stillness will it come.

Christ does not destroy flesh and blood. In communion with him there is no room for alienation. He does not break what is within us. He has come not to destroy but to fulfil. When you listen, in the silence of your heart, he transfigures all that troubles you most. When you are shrouded in what you cannot understand, when darkness gathers, his love is a flame. You need only fix your gaze on that lamp burning in the darkness, till day begins to dawn and the sun rises in your heart.

Brother Roger of Taizé, *Parable of Communion*.

CHAPTER 3

Praying with music

'When we sing we pray twice.' So said St Augustine. In general people don't sing in the churches in Ireland. This is sad because it deprives liturgy and worship of a vibrancy and power that singing and music can bring. Cardinal Ó Fiaich told the Extraordinary Synod in Rome some years ago that the Irish will sing away in the pub but not in the church. It's one of our many eccentricities!

Singing and music in general are very powerful ways of praying. Throughout this book I make the point that words are often not the best vehicle for praying. For the heart-to-heart world of prayer there are other lines of communication and expression that can be more beneficial and more powerful. Music communicates on levels that resonate with something deep within. Some years ago a space probe was launched which carried material that might someday be found by any possible life-forms out in the cosmos. Part of this material was a collection of pieces of music through which it was hoped to communicate something of the human character and spirit where words might prove useless.

Music has a power of its own. It can express any mood. It can soothe us, calm us down, bring us to quiet. It can excite patriotic passions and great drive. While I was at college, I had a chance to visit the south of Italy with a friend. We went to the Basilica at Bari in the crypt of which is the shrine and Orthodox chapel of St Nicholas of Myra. As we went down the first steps we heard a gentle singing, almost a kind of keening. At first we thought it was some background taped music but as we got down into the crypt we saw an old woman at the shrine swaying away and singing softly to herself. She was praying and we felt ashamed at disturbing this beautiful and most sincere of prayers.

Professor Breandán Ó Madagáin of University College Galway has written and spoken of how the Irish in the last century and further back used to compose and sing their prayers and their invocations. Often this talent for instant composition was used for attack and satire, but it was also used for praying! If we listen to modern music, some of it can be seen as a prayer of modern culture and the modern world. So much modern music expresses the themes and concerns of young people. It is their vehicle, often bringing out their hopes and dreams, their disappointments and fears. Lots of it can be glib and packaged for certain markets, but there are some very serious musicians out there who write and sing lyrics that meet many people's attempts at praying more than half-way. The list is endless but Tracy Chapman, Suzanne Vega, U2, Bob Dylan, Van Morrison, Dolores Keane, Jimmy McCarthy, Mary Black, Christy Moore, Bruce Springsteen, Paul Simon, Sinéad O Connor are just some of the names that come to mind. In seeking to become more reflective people, and in seeking to put words and images on what may be going on inside us, there is no reason why modern music cannot find a place in our prayer, why it cannot feed our quieter times.

For Irish people, a slow air or the sounds of the flute or pipes can draw something out of them that is not easy to explain. In church, a traditional air nearly always seems to bring a special hush and peace. Many people of Irish descent, and many who have tasted Irish life and culture, feel this special spirituality in Irish music. As a background to our prayer and as a way of coming to quiet, using a piece from the tradition is very helpful. It can even offer a moment of prayer itself if we allow it to carry us. The likes of Micheál Ó Súilleabháin, Seán and Peadar Ó Riada, Davy Spillane, Shaun Davey, Enya, Nóirín Ní Riain and the Monks of Glenstal, Moving Hearts, Dé Danann, the Chieftains have all recorded pieces that might help in our prayer.

The music of Taizé deserves a mention here. In the liturgy and prayer at Taizé, music plays a powerful role. By using short chants in Latin and many different languages, many people have been helped to come to a deepness of prayer and quietness. The repetition of a phrase has been suggested elsewhere. Allowing music and that repeated phrase to go together can be very powerful. The phrases are familiar phrases but they have a depth that can be explored again and again and never be exhausted. They are an incredibly rich form of prayer. Different recordings of the music of Taizé exist and many prayer groups use the music and chants for their prayer. You will also find available recordings of Gregorian chant and other traditional forms of Church music.

Over the years many folk groups have been formed in parishes and schools and their music has added a life and a depth to the Church that many people have come to value. There are many, many pieces of music that have come from this movement; at this stage the better ones seem to be finding a place. Joining or forming such a group in your own area might be one way of integrating your prayer and your life in a very worthwhile way.

Finally, you might actually start to do something practical to use music a little bit more in your prayer and reflection. Start listening to lyrics and find a singer or a group that seem to say something to you. Maybe they are expressing things that are half-buried within you and which you find difficult to express. There is no reason why this music or these lyrics shouldn't find a place in your prayer.

You may also like to use some instrumental music in your prayer. This music might help to bring you to pray. Play a piece and follow its mood. Allow it to carry you. Help your moods and the ups and downs of life to come more into focus by allowing the music to express what might be deep inside. Even in the prayer time itself some quiet music in the background may help you.

Music really has a power all of its own and it speaks to us on levels that are very familiar to our attempts at prayer. In the wonder that is the cosmos, music is a true universal language: it lifts us and carries us in a very powerful way when it comes to praying.

CHAPTER 4

Praying with the environment

Being someway in tune with the world around us offers a place for praying and a way of praying that can have a very special power. Music can bring us down roads where words fail. Being able to walk the earth and feel it beneath our feet can open up the world of the heart in its own way. The mountains, the sea, running water, the wind in the trees, the mists, the changing seasons – all these resonate with our lives and our experience. There's great power in the world around us; there is a ferocity and an intensity that can be terrifying. There's also great gentleness and a soothing character to the earth, the air and water. To watch a sunset, to see the waves lapping on the shore, to watch animals with their young; if we have time for these things and an eye to take them in, we have something precious.

God is everywhere in this world that carries his footprints. It is holy ground. Time and time again in the Bible, God is present in the elements and is mirrored in creation. For anyone who knows the Kerry hills God can seem to be especially mirrored in the mist, as Noel Dermot O Donoghue has noted. The mist moves, it flows, it covers and it reveals. Sometimes all is mysterious and hidden, then suddenly the bulk of the mountain is revealed in all its solidness. Sometimes the view is clear and then suddenly the mist comes down and we can see no further than our outstretched hand. We are teased and tantalised, we are promised wonders and sights we can sometimes only speculate about. Then, in a matter of moments, the vista opens out before us.

When I was ordained to the priesthood, I put a particular scene on the front of my ordination commemoration card. Using Celtic spirals and simple lines, the mountains, the sea and an early cross-motif from a slab in West Kerry were depicted. There is a rootedness to the mountains that one is very conscious of in a place like this, just as there are some things in life which endure, things which are always fixed and on which we depend. There is also the ebb and flow of the sea; life too has its ebb and flow, there is a lack of certainty and a degree of the unknown and the unexpected about all we do. Somewhere in the middle of all of this, drawing the two together, is the presence of Christ. In the Kerry landscape, the old monastic sites and cross-slabs stand between the mountains and the sea. Between the things that are rooted in life and the constant flux life brings, Christ and the gospel are present. The world around us in all its grandeur can teach us this.

Not everyone is blessed to live in the paradise that is south-west Ireland! All of us however can find special places which are our points of meeting with our creator God. It may be a country lane or a harbour wall. It may be a corner in a city park or in the back garden. It may be on the side of a mountain or by the side of the sea, or a river. It may simply be a dreamed-of place away from our concrete jungle. It's important to have it. It is in this place that the world of the heart can come alive in a special way.

An exercise that you could do is to close your eyes and to travel to this place. It may only be a place remembered from a holiday or a film. It may also be a place that you know very well. Travel there in your mind and feel the power and presence of this place. Empty yourself of all the baggage, the business, the weight of your daily burdens. There is no need for them here. Just be at peace. You share this place with the God who is there before you. This is your meeting place, your secret place, a place loved by you both and which is special to you. Speak to God here, allow his presence in this place to speak to you. Take it all in, every detail, every sign of its life. Make it a special place, a place you can always go to.

In the early Irish Church we find a tremendous richness of personal and nature poetry. All around the country are dotted the remains in stone of small monasteries and hermitages. The monastery of Skellig Michael and the hermitage on the same island cling to the side of a rock out in the Atlantic. Other monasteries and hermitages are in more accessible places but many of them are in locations of great natural beauty. The earliest monks in Egypt and the Middle East found their desert and sought to unite themselves with God in prayer there. Many of the Irish monks found their own deserts in remote places or on the offshore islands in the desert of the sea. Some too went further afield. The story of Brendan is the great epic of this movement but evidence of the travels of Irish monks is found in the islands of Scotland, in Iceland and maybe even beyond. They too had their sense of journey and pilgrimage and the God of Creation was central to this. The Celtic and early Irish world was a world of great balance and great power in nature. Some verses from the tradition illustrate this very well, showing the quest and the importance of direct contact with the world around the writers.

A wall of forest looms above
and sweetly the blackbird sings;
all the birds make melody
over me and my books and things.

There sings to me the cuckoo
from bush-citadels in grey hood.
God's doom! May the Lord protect me
writing well, under the great wood.

(from James Carney, *Medieval Irish Lyrics*, Dolmen Press 1985.)

Learned in music sings the lark,
I leave my cell to listen;
His open beak spills music, hark!
Where heaven's bright cloudlets glisten.

And so I'll sing my morning psalm
That God bright Heaven may give me
And keep me in eternal calm
And from all sin relieve me.

(from Patrick Murray (ed.) , *The Deer's Cry*, Four Courts Press, 1986.)

I wish, O Son of the living God,
O ancient, eternal King,
For a hidden little hut in the wilderness
That it may be my dwelling.

An all-grey lithe little lark
To be by its side,
A clear pool to wash away sins
Through the grace of the Holy Spirit.

Quite near, a beautiful wood,
Around it on every side,
To nurse many-voiced birds,
Hiding it with its shelter.

And I to be sitting for a while
praying God in every place.

(from Patrick Murray (ed.) , *The Deer's Cry*, Four Courts Press,
1986.)

Another collection of texts like these is found in David Greene
and Frank O Connor, *A Golden Treasury of Irish Poetry, A.D. 600-
1200*, Reprinted by Brandon, 1990. Frank O Connor's *Kings, Lords
and Commons* has also been reprinted recently (Gill & Macmillan,
1991). *Saltair* (ed. P. Ó Fiannachta & Desmond Forristal, Columba
Press, 1990) contains a selection of prayers and translations from
the Irish tradition.

CHAPTER 5

Praying with the Cross

The Cross is real. There is no denying the reality of suffering and pain in the world. Many people carry an intolerable burden of sickness, stress and bereavement. They suffer great oppression for their beliefs, colour or race. People cave in under the pressures of family life and modern living. People seek refuge in drink, drugs and easy pleasure. To be human is to know the Cross and so often the cry of 'why' or 'how long?' rises to heaven.

We speak of a God of love and yet we see such misery. There are appalling natural and man-made disasters. Children die from illness and in accidents. Sometimes the human spirit seems all but crushed. Sometimes it is crushed. Surely there must be an answer, a reason. Sometimes we wonder if there can be a God at all. A questioning of God and his ways often comes early to all those who suffer.

There is a mysterious, hidden side to suffering. Sometimes people come through it and overcome the fiercest of odds. It draws families and communities together in the strongest of bonds and leads to great solidarity and self-sacrifice. This cannot, however, explain suffering away or make it acceptable. That would be something too horrendous to contemplate. A world where we are purified through suffering? Who has this as a priority? What kind of a world would this be? A world where God allows suffering, a God who in some mysterious way brings us through it to a newness of life - all this, yes, but to believe this requires a huge leap of faith, an enormous fund of trust in God. Suffering has a place in God's plan of salvation but God is a God who has shared in our suffering, rather than a God who wishes suffering on us.

It is only by going to Jesus that we can even begin to explore the mystery of suffering. Perhaps it is only in the Cross that we can find some clue, that we can make some sense of it all. In Jesus we have God's great act of solidarity and compassion with human-kind. Jesus was spared nothing. He endured the most horrible of deaths. He was rejected. He lost all the goodwill he had built up. In just a week they changed from wanting to make him king to mocking him and jeering as he died. Even his closest followers couldn't seem to understand. Only the very few, largely women, kept faith with him and stayed with him. All was finished. All he could do was trust in his Father. How difficult that must have been!

Because of the Cross, however, because of the death of Jesus, the stranglehold of death and suffering is somehow broken. Love has been shown to be more powerful than death and love will endure. In the horror of the Cross is the triumph of love and the promise of a God who will never leave us or abandon us to our pain. The Cross is the ultimate bridge between us and God.

Elie Wiesel survived the death camps of Nazi Germany and has striven ever since to remind the world that an evil such as this ac-tually happened. He describes, in his book 'Night', an incident where a young child was hanged after an act of sabotage. He was hanged with two others and, as the heads were placed in the noose, a voice cried out, 'Where is God? Where is he?' After it was over the same voice continued to ask the same question. A voice within Elie Wiesel answered, 'Here he is – he is hanging here on this gallows ...'

The Cross reminds us that God does not remain aloof. God is with us in our suffering. God does not plan it or wish it. Suffering is there. It is part of the mystery we do not yet understand. Christ walks ahead of us on this road. He walks with us. He knows this road well. His way was the way of the Cross. After the Second World War some philosophers and theologians began to wonder how we could continue to believe in God after all the horror the world had experienced. How could we pray? How could we pray after Auschwitz? A German theologian who examined this quest-ion remarked in a dialogue with a philosopher that the only reason we could continue to pray after Auschwitz was that people prayed in Auschwitz. God was in Auschwitz just as he continues to be in jails and personal prisons worldwide. God does not create this, he did not build Auschwitz. Yet he was there.

To pray in front of the Cross, to pray with the crucified Christ, is a powerful and meaningful way to pray. In the Eastern Churches they gather around the Cross. Often it is placed on the floor and those who wish may approach it, lay their heads on it and join in prayer with the crucified Christ.

If you have a special corner or place for prayer, you might keep a Cross. When you pray before it you join in solidarity with all those who suffer and with the Christ who keeps vigil with them. In praying in this way you can come to lay your burdens before Christ, who takes them to himself, who goes before us on every way of the Cross. Remember too all those who suffer. Pray for those you know by name. Think too of all the forgotten ones, in shanty towns and prisons, remembered only by Christ. The Cross is our point of contact with the God who loves to the point of laying down his life. It is our sign of unity with a suffering Church.

Charles de Foucauld, who died as a hermit in the Sahara and inspired a number of groups to live as he did, has a prayer which has often been described as the prayer of abandonment. It might well be the prayer of the crucified Christ. It is the prayer of all who, in the face of everything, abandon themselves to the Father. To abandon oneself totally can be the most difficult thing of all, to have that faith, that hope, that love. 'Father, into your hands I commend my spirit.' May we, by following the road of Jesus, come to that moment of abandonment and have no hesitation to trust. It can cost 'not less than everything', but it is perhaps the greatest invitation we will ever receive.

> Father,
> I abandon myself into your hands;
> do with me what you will.
> Whatever you may do I thank you;

I am ready for all, I accept all.
Let only your will be done in me,
and in all your creatures.
I wish no more than this, O Lord.
Into your hands I commend my spirit;
I offer it to you,
with all the love of my heart,
for I love you, Lord,
and so need to give myself,
to surrender myself into your hands,
without reserve,
and with boundless confidence,
for you are my Father.
(Charles de Foucauld)

O living God,
you no longer knew how to express to human beings
that you are nothing but love and forgiveness,
that you never want suffering for anyone on the
earth, that you never punish.
And so to make yourself understood,
you came on earth in poverty,
through your Christ.
Now, risen from the dead, Christ Jesus is present by his Spirit
in every person,
he is there for those who suffer trials.
As we advance with you, one day we shall tell you:
sing in me O Christ,
your love has burnt into my soul.
(Brother Roger of Taizé, *Praying Together in Word and Song*).

The way of the Cross, the Stations, has always been a popular
devotion. There is power and drama in them. In most Churches
you will find a Stations of the Cross. You can make your own way
of the Cross by following them. You might like to take a gospel
account and follow the way of Jesus to Calvary. As you do,
whether it is by following the representation on the wall or the
words of the gospel, make it your own. The trial, the judgement,

the scourging, the falls, the mocking, the stripping, the terrible end. These are familiar things. We may never have to endure as Jesus did, but in a thousand ways we can find moments in our lives and the lives of others that gel with this hour of Jesus. There are so many people the world over who can identify exactly with each station, with each moment and event on the way. We can reach out to them in our prayer and our solidarity with Jesus.

In the chapter on 'Prayer and Life' I mention possibilities for action on behalf of the oppressed. Those who work with *Amnesty International* will tell you what a single letter of support, a message of good wishes from far away, can mean to someone behind bars or someone who has all but disappeared from normal life. Can we sit idly by while so many of our sisters and brothers suffer? Must we not at least reach out to them in the heart-talk world of prayer? It does make a difference, perhaps the difference that at the end of the day will count most. Maybe we can change very little of a crazy, often rotten world. We can at least join that pilgrimage of all who suffer, walking the way with the Christ who gave his life for us.

CHAPTER 6

Praying with the Risen Christ

Together with the whole people of God, with people from all over the world, you are invited to live a life exceeding all your hopes. On your own, how could you ever experience the radiance of God's presence?

God is too dazzling to be looked upon. He is a God who blinds our sight. It is Christ who channels this consuming fire, and allows God to shine through without dazzling us.

Christ is present, close to each one of us, whether we know him or not. He is so bound up with us that he lives within us, even when we are unaware of him. He is there in secret, a fire burning in the heart, a light in the darkness. But Christ is also someone other than yourself. He is alive; he stands beyond, ahead of you. Here is his secret: he loved you first.

(Brother Roger of Taize, *A Life We Never Dared Hope For* .)

Again and again in this book, we meet with the person of Christ, we find him on the road, we see the light he brings. The heart of the Christian faith and message is a person. This is the secret that can remain hidden. We can go to the Bible and find many passages that offer challenge and hope. It would be a terrible thing if we were to miss the fact that, at the heart of it all, is a person. In Christ we experience the fullness of God's love and revelation. Many other things can be pillars of the Christian life but without Christ at the heart it is empty.

The Church and the Christian community, the life of the gospel and the teachings of the Church, the Bible itself; all these are centred on Christ, on the Risen Christ. At the very core is the proclamation, 'Christ has died, Christ is risen, Christ will come again.'

But on the first day of the week, at early dawn, they went to the tomb, taking spices which they had prepared. And they found the stone rolled away from the tomb, but when they went in they did not find the body. While they were perplexed about this, behold, two men stood by them in dazzling apparel; and as they were frightened and bowed their faces to the ground, the men said to them, 'Why do you seek the living amongst the dead? He is not here, but has risen. Remember how he told you, while he was still in Galilee, that the Son of man must be delivered into the hands of sinful men, and be crucified, and on the third day rise.' And they remembered his words.
(Lk 24:1-8)

Why look among the dead for someone who is alive? Jesus is not here. He has risen. Who do you say that I am? We are often told that we are Easter people, that we carry the message of Easter in our hearts and lives and that out of the empty tomb comes the hope of eternal life. Saying this and believing this are two different things!

When it comes to the ceremonies of Easter week, the celebration of the passion, death and resurrection of Jesus, it seems that the Good Friday liturgy strikes a chord with us in a very real way. The Cross is real for so many people, pain and suffering are familiar fellow-travellers on the road of life. It's not that we celebrate or rejoice in the Cross, but the reading of the passion, the starkness of the occasion and the suffering of Jesus do resonate with us. The liturgy explodes with joy on Holy Saturday night. There is a huge richness and wealth of symbol, but is there the same resonance without life-experience?

Thomas Merton wrote of how people seem to have little difficulty going into the tomb with Jesus but have great difficulty coming out. Jesus is not here. Yet it seems that the darkness is more familiar than the light. All of life, all of history, is flooded in the light of that first Easter morning. Death and the darkness of sin have been conquered and they must give way. How easy to say, but how difficult to believe!

The question asked again and again of us is, 'Who do you say that I am?' In our prayer we come in all our poverty, our lack of faith, our business and our burdens; we come to that Risen Lord. We come again and again so that we can come to say in our hearts, 'You are the Christ. You are the one longed for, the one who suffered, died and rose. The one who will come again. You are the one we long for now, the one who has loved us first and the one we often cannot see already present before us.'

'Christ has a word to say to you, a personal and direct word, in which is contained the secret of your present and future. If you know how to welcome it, you will be able to walk safely and happily to meet your future.' (Pope John Paul)

The community at Taizé is a community that dares to live and grow without the barriers that keep the Christian traditions apart. They live a life of reconciliation, a life very close to the Risen Christ. They open that life to many people and to young people in particular. They invite those who come to Taizé to travel with them on a pilgrimage of trust in the Risen Lord, daring to hope, daring to believe that there is a life beyond what we could ever imagine.

The following are some prayers from *Praying Together in Word and Song*, which is published by Mowbray, London.

O Christ,
tirelessly you seek out those who are looking for you
and who think that you are far away;
teach us, at every moment,
to place our spirits in your hands.
While we are still looking for you,
already you have found us.
However poor our prayer,
you hear us far more than we can imagine or believe.

Risen Christ,
today, tomorrow and always,
your Spirit lives in us.
Sometimes we feel we understand so little.
But remaining in your presence, wherever we are,
is prayer.
And perhaps close to you, O Christ,
silence is often everything in prayer.
And then we sense that, our whole life long,
we advance when trust in you guides every step,
when a trusting heart is at the beginning of everything.

Lord Christ,
had we faith enough to move mountains,
without love
what would we be?
But you love us.
Without your Spirit who lives in our hearts,
what would we be?
But you love us.
Taking everything upon yourself,
you open for us a way towards the peace of God,
who wants neither suffering nor human distress.
Spirit of the Risen Christ.
Spirit of compassion, Spirit of praise,
your love for each one of us
will never fail.

In following you, O Christ,
we choose to love and not to harden our hearts,
even when the incomprehensible happens.
As we remain in your presence with perseverance,
day after day, and pray with simplicity of heart,
you come and make us into people
who are a leaven of confident trust by the way we live.
And all that your Gospel calls us to,
all that you ask of us, you give.

O living God,
in our darkness you kindle a fire that never dies out.
Through the spirit of praise, you take us out of ourselves.
To us, the poor of God, you have entrusted a mystery of hope.
In our human frailty,
you have set a spiritual strength that is never withdrawn.
Even when we are unaware of it, it is always there,
ready to carry us onward.
Yes, in our darkness, you kindle a fire that never dies out.

Christ Jesus, by your Spirit
you come and kindle a burning light in us.
We know well that it is not we
who create this source of light,
but you the Risen Lord.
To all of us, you give the one thing that matters
and which is hidden from our own eyes:
a peaceful trust in God
and also poverty in spirit,
so that with a great thirst for the realities of God,
we may take the risk of letting you accompany us
O Christ,
and of accompanying, in our turn,
those whom you entrust to us.

Why not use these prayers as part of Morning or Night Prayer, perhaps as a concluding prayer? You may also like to use one of them for a time of prayer, praying it line by line and letting its words and power flow in and out of your life.

Other collections of texts from Taizé include *His Love is a Fire* (Br Roger, Geoffrey Chapman Mowbray, 1990) and *No Greater Love* (Br Roger, Geoffrey Chapman Mowbray, 1991).

CHAPTER 7

Prayer and life

And what does the Lord require of you but to do justice, and to love kindness, and to walk humbly with your God? (Micah 6:8)

What does it profit, my brethren, if a man says he has faith but has not works? Can his faith save him? If a brother or sister is ill-clad and in lack of daily food, and one of you says to them, 'Go in peace, be warmed and filled,' without giving them the things needed for the body, what does it profit? So faith by itself , if it has no works, is dead. (James 2:14-17)

There was a particularly heavy wave of bombing at one point during the Korean war. One of the casualties in this attack was a Church. When the priest went to check the damage he saw that the statue of Christ had been badly damaged. The face was quite mutilated and the hands and feet had been blown off. Some soldiers came by and offered to get the statue fixed. The priest thought for a moment and then said, 'No, I will leave it the way it is. I'll make out a sign for it instead with the words:

I have no eyes but yours to see with,
no ears but yours to hear with,
no hands but yours to work and care with,
no feet but yours to walk in the world.

No man or woman is an island, we say. We live our lives in relationship to others. We live in a world where it always seems that the rich get richer and the poor get poorer. There is so much poverty of spirit as well. Many people seem to have intolerable burdens. Our prayer can never be divorced from life. Prayer and life must flow in and out of each other. There is always the invitation and the challenge to be a leaven of peace, understanding and compassion in the world in which we live.

Maybe changing the whole world is beyond us but changing our own world is not. Even the tiniest of candles when lit banishes the darkness; a thousand, a million such candles would push it further and further away. There are very public ways of integrating our prayer and our life and there are also quite private ways which are just as important. To be a wellspring of reconciliation and understanding, to be someone who encourages and supports, these can be real challenges. There are so many who tear down, who wait to criticise and knock, who spread a gospel of malice and selfishness. Our contribution may often only mean a quiet word or a smile. These in their own way can make such a difference! Wherever we are, at home, in school, at work, the call of the gospel is the call to let our light shine out!

In the gospel, Jesus often poses a simple question which is staggering in its implications. One such question is found in Chapter 6 of John's gospel. In the incident of the miracle of the loaves, Jesus asks Philip, 'Where can we buy some bread for these people to eat?' Such a simple question but such a question for our world today! There is enough for everyone to eat but so many are denied such a basic necessity. As Christians, what can we do? What questions should we be asking? What demands might it make on our lives?

Further on in John's gospel, we find a different account of the Last Supper and the institution of the Eucharist from the ones found in the other gospels or in Paul. Instead we get the account of the washing of the feet of the disciples. For John, the Eucharist and service of others, real service, are absolutely linked. Washing someone's feet is a menial job, one reserved for slaves or the lowest of servants in Jesus' day. By doing this very task Jesus has left us a powerful sign of what our faith must lead us to do. There is a radical nature to this service which should never be diluted. The enthusiasm we first enjoy, both of youth and the gospel, can easily be worn away by the pressures of living and the ways of society. The gospel is not for revolution in a sense which destroys and simply adds to people's misery, but the call of the gospel is still a radical one.

Answering this call may lead some to join or work with development and justice groups like Concern, Oxfam, Trócaire, Amnesty International and so on. It may encourage local justice and peace groups in schools and parishes. It may invite actions of witness and solidarity. These may sometimes carry their own price. It is of course not necessary to join groups and organisations although it is difficult to know if we can simply sit idly by while there is suffering, starvation and injustice on such a huge scale in our world.

Our daily living, our willingness to listen and to care, our understanding and compassion, these too are signs of our response. If all of us would really care for just one other person, wouldn't that alone transform our world? That care might not be easy. It might not bring much by way of reward or response here and now. That too is simply part of it. We don't love so that others will love us. We love because we are already loved by God and this love calls for a response.

At the end of the day, we always have a chance to look back over the day, to look back at the pattern of our life that day and our encounters with others. We are told never to let the sun go down on our anger. Maybe this can be widened so that we end the day at peace with our world. Tomorrow is always a new day. There are ways in which we could do better. Maybe we need to forgive or to try to understand or to ask forgiveness. We often might feel that others don't understand us. Dare we try always to put understanding others first? How have we been the hands and eyes and mouth of Christ this day? How can we make a renewed effort, a new beginning?

It would be wrong to feel the burden of failures, and lack of response to Christ in the lives we lead, to the extent that we load ourselves with guilt and self-criticism. Instead we should see each day as an invitation to love, to build bridges, to understand and show kindness and encouragement. Sometimes there are things to regret but instead of letting this cripple us we should learn from our patient God who always offers the chance of a new beginning. The letter of John says, 'We may love because God loved us first.' Our love is our response to that loving God.

Praying for others and for the world

To pray for others and for our world is important and powerful, to let good thoughts and wishes flow out of us, bringing our peace and earnest prayer for the world to touch others of goodwill. In the Bible the word of God is active. It goes forth and it goes to work. Once sent forth it does not return and it has an edge to it which brings about change. There is plenty of ill-will in the world, plenty of hate, pain, anger, envy and greed. All of us have our part to play in praying for our fellow human beings and for a better world. We are all invited to counter all that tears people down and weighs heavily on the world by the peace and hope that rests in our hearts. We want a better world and we want to hold those we love and care for in our hands outstretched before the Lord. Having a special time of intercession for our world is something powerful which each one of us can do.

In doing this we just sit with the Lord, coming to quiet in his presence. Then in the stillness we can begin to pray, to hold those we love before him, to ask a blessing, or healing, or peace. We name them one by one and ask that the Holy Spirit come down on them. We also pray for those who suffer, for the sick, the oppressed, the marginalised, the lonely, the elderly, the dying. It helps to make the prayer specific, to think of a person or a group or a situation. We also pray for those who seek to serve these people, who strive to be the hands, feet, eyes, mouth and ears of the Christ who is present in all the poor and is present to them all. We pray too for our own poverty and ask for the blessedness that this poverty can bring us. We pray for those who have died, those who have gone no further than God who is very near. Pray for them by name and hold any precious memory you have. We also pray for the world and the creation God has placed in our hands.

The following are some suggestions. For some, few words will be needed; for others it will help to talk, to open torrents of feeling and emotion, to pour out the heart.

You may like to come to quiet first or you may like to begin by using a general prayer. This prayer could be the Our Father, a decade of the Rosary or you could draw on the collections of prayers found in different places in this book.

1. Lord, I ask you to bless and show your care to those whom I love, those who show me the warmth and strength of their love and support. I pray for … (*name them, think of them, pray for any special situation affecting them*). Show them that you hold each one of us in the palm of your hand. Grant them your peace and fill them with hope. Help us all to grow in love of each other and love of you. Help us to listen to each other, to listen to each other's stories and the ups and downs of life and help us to be always there for each other.

2. Lord, all over the world people light flickering candles of hope to banish the darkness. People search to find you and seek to make your kingdom come in an infinity of places and lives. Help us all in our pilgrimage through life. Guide the Church, the gathering of frail and timid believers. Help our leaders and all who serve in the Church. Guide those who seek to follow you in lives of prayer and care of others. Help us to witness in our daily lives to you and to bring you to all those we meet each day.

3. Lord, I pray for all those who suffer. I pray for my brothers and sisters who suffer because of their witness to you and to the gospel. (*Think of some situations*). Be close to those who are sick and those who care for refugees and those who have to endure famine and the destruction of natural disasters. Help me to seek you out among the poor and those who are pushed to the margins. Keep me close to the poverty of my own life because it is there that you are to be found.

4. Lord, help us to work for a better world. Guide all leaders and people of wealth and power to seek to end all that wears people down and causes misery and hardship. Help us to end all wars, to seek the peace that only you can bring in the midst of conflict and lack of understanding. Teach us to be people of patience and openness and to learn from the life of the gospel which teaches us the unique dignity and worth possessed by every person. Help us to be close to the simple things that bind us all together and not to be consumed by all that can glitter in the world of success and power.

5. Lord, I pray for our world, your gift which you have entrusted to us. Help us to care for the earth, to walk barefoot on it in our hearts, to feel the surge of creation and its immense beauty. Teach us to realise that we have a duty to our world and to those who will come after us. Help us to preserve what speaks to the heart and sings of your love for us and the wonder that everything around us can hint at. Teach us wisdom in developing and planning the future and help us not to sacrifice the future for what seems immediately desirable.

6. Lord, I pray for this local community, this district/ parish/ town. I pray for its families and for their worries and cares. I pray for the children and young people. Help us to give them witness and example, to give them a sense of their own worth and to give them promise of a life of hope and fulfilment. May this local community be a people of trust and welcome, a people going out to each other and gathering to the heart all who live and come here. Protect those who work the land, who work in factories and services. Help us to treasure our old people and to learn from their wisdom and experience.

7. Lord, gather to yourself those who have died, I pray especially for ... (*name and think of those you would like to pray for*). May they find in your presence light, happiness and peace. May any faults of this life be washed away in the tide of your love and forgiveness. Help us all to find our way home, to endure the journey and to keep our hearts and eyes set on the promise of eternal life in the fullness of time.

There are so many things to pray for! Use and adapt the above to suit. On occasions it is enough to take just one of the above and to spend the whole time with this prayer or even a line of it, drawing it out and thinking of all it brings with it. The Lord tells us to ask and we will receive, to seek and we shall find, to knock and the door will be opened. Above all he asks us to have faith – even the tiniest glimmer sincerely held has the power to move mountains. We must be careful of only one thing and that is not to have the answer to our prayer made out even before we pray! Our prayer will be answered but it may not be answered in the way that we have decided it should be answered! That belongs to God. He will not fail us.

CHAPTER 9

Praying with Mary

Mary our mother is the great figure of hope ... Mary is the final image of the Church. One creature – and one creature alone – has broken the barrier between earth and heaven. One creature is already in that state, outside time, outside space where all of us, one day, hope to be. Mary is there and we will follow. One ship has rounded the headland. We are the little ships following her home.

(Archbishop Joseph Cassidy, Irish Youth Pilgrimage to Rome, 1981.)

The Mother of God occupies a special place in the hearts of Catholics. We sometimes think that Mary, being like all mothers, will always have the welcome and the kind word, that she will slip us in the back door when we feel that on our own we just can't make it. Maybe that's a sign of our lack of faith in the Father but we know that mothers are like that.

I have spoken of the pilgrim Christ who walks the way with us through life. Mary also has had her pilgrimage. Sometimes she is presented as a weak, humble, almost insipid individual. That she could never have been. In the Temple Simeon prophesied that a sword would pierce her heart too. How she must have struggled and suffered as she watched her Son during those years of public life and the end it brought. The young woman, maybe only still a young girl, who listened to the words of Gabriel; what must she have thought! Yet she said, 'Yes.' She had to say that 'yes' again and again; the woman who was the first missionary, carrying the child within her and the Good News to her cousin Elizabeth; the woman of the *Magnificat*, a song of joy and of promise, a song that outlined a programme of events that could turn the world on its head.

My soul proclaims the greatness of the Lord
and my spirit exults in God my saviour;
because he has looked upon his lowly handmaid.
Yes, from this day forward all generations will call me blessed,
for the Almighty has done great things for me.
Holy is his name,
and his mercy reaches from age to age for those who fear him.
He has shown the power of his arm,
he has routed the proud of heart.
He has pulled down princes from their thrones and exalted the
lowly.
The hungry he has filled with good things, the rich sent empty
away.
He has come to the help of Israel his servant, mindful of his
mercy
- according to the promise he made to our ancestors -
of his mercy to Abraham and to his descendants for ever.

Mary, the woman of the gospel, one of those who remained faithful, who believed even when she held her dead son in her arms; the woman who was able to witness to his resurrection and to the coming of the Holy Spirit. Mary has become the mother of all Christians in a special way. We know the Mary of Lourdes, Fatima and Knock. We are now coming to know her as Our Lady of Czestochowa and Mother of the Church in Eastern Europe. Mary has been with us down through the ages as Mother of the Church and many people believe that she has appeared in times of great poverty, tension and difficulty.

The Marian shrines are special places. I find no difficulty in believing that Mary appeared there. This may be a scandal for some Christians but Mary does not have to be a sign of division. In the past Mary was somehow put on a level with Christ if that is the right way to put it. There might have been the temptation to find in Mary the human face, the understanding mother, the one who might understand better. The women's movement has taught us to see the feminine in God, however, and we have learned too to see the all-encompassing mercy and gentle love of God. Mary points to Jesus. It was so in the beginning at the feast at Cana. It is so today. 'Through Mary to Jesus' is how they put it in Lourdes. How Mary must long to bring us to her Son.

She has rounded the headland, she is home.

> Mary, Mother of the Church, you are our hope, the sign of God's promise. You were the first to believe and through your 'yes' to God, Jesus came into the world. Help us to say 'yes' to him too so that through us he will truly be present to all people, especially those in need of his peace.

The Rosary has been a very special prayer for many centuries. Many young people seem to have turned off it. And yet it is so much part of our tradition, so much part of our family life and of family unity and togetherness. As prayer, the Rosary brings together the major events in the life, death and resurrection of Christ and the beginnings of the Church and the place of Mary in that Church.

I have drawn attention to the great value repetition of simple prayers can have. The Rosary makes use of this to offer a meditation on Mary and on faith in Christ. The simple repetition, the thumbing of the beads, have been so much part of us for so long, it would be a shame to see the Rosary almost ignored. It doesn't have to be the only form of prayer and for some families in particular there may be problems in getting children to say it. It might be enough to just say one decade well and to use a bit of Scripture or some prayers.

When you come to say the Rosary or even a part of it, keep one eye on the Scriptures, on the texts that are relevant to the particular mystery. You may integrate saying the Rosary with reading and praying the Scripture, meditating on what the mystery remembers as you say it.

We have fifteen decades in all. These are usually grouped in three sets of five. These are the Joyful, the Sorrowful and the Glorious Mysteries.

The Joyful Mysteries:
The Annunciation of the Angel Gabriel.
The Visitation of Mary to Elizabeth.
The Nativity of Jesus.
The Presentation in the Temple.
The Finding of Jesus in the Temple.

The Sorrowful Mysteries:
The Agony in the Garden.
The Scourging at the Pillar.
The Crowning with Thorns.
The Carrying of the Cross.
The Crucifixion.

The Glorious Mysteries:
The Resurrection.
The Ascension.
The Coming of the Holy Spirit.
The Assumption of Our Lady into Heaven.
Our Lady, Queen of Heaven.

Evening/Night Prayer

We end the day as we began:

In the name of the Father, the Son and the Holy Spirit.

Once again, no matter how the day has gone or what it has brought, we give thanks and praise to the God who was with us during the day, the God whose blessing we asked on all that we would do. We say, as we did in the morning:

Glory be to the Father and to the Son and to the Holy Spirit. As it was in the beginning, is now and ever shall be world without end. Amen.

We now take a few moments to draw the day together, to think back over the different events and to remember the people we met. There might be one or two difficult situations we want to place before the Lord or one or two people we would like to pray for in a special way. Name them and ask for their needs.

A short examination of the day could be done now too.

What good did you do this day?

Were there moments of special consideration or listening, a time when you went out of your way for someone?

What were the happy moments, the times of laughter and fun, the moments of friendship and love?

Was there a special time of closeness to God or a time when you felt his presence?

Maybe there is some anger or hurt there. Can you name it and place it in outstretched hands before the Lord?

Can you ask his healing and peace?

Can you resolve to try and bring peace tomorrow to that situation?

Think back over anything that you have done that showed a lack of love or peace or understanding or forgiveness.

Were there ways in which you were selfish?
Were there ways in which you manipulated or used anyone?
Did you talk about anyone behind their backs or take from their good name?
Were you honest in all your dealings?
Can you forgive others anything you need to forgive?

Sit with the day that is nearly over, be honest about it and talk it over. Make a promise that you won't let the sun go down on any anger and that where you need to try again you will do so. Ask the Lord's pardon and promise you will make a fresh start tomorrow in any way you need to. The Lord will not store up anything against you. You are precious to him and he believes in you. Open the day to him and be at peace.

O my God, I am heartily sorry for all my sins
because they offend you who are infinitely good.
I firmly resolve with the help of your grace,
never more to offend you and to amend my life.
Amen.

or

O my God, I love you.
I am sorry for my sins,
for not loving others and not loving you.
Help me to live like Jesus and not to sin again.
Amen.

We have already used the prayer of Charles de Foucauld, the Prayer of Abandonment. No matter how the day has gone, we can gather it together and place it in God's hands.

Father, I abandon myself into your hands;
do with me what you will.
Whatever you may do I thank you;
I am ready for all, I accept all.
Let only your will be done in me,

and in all your creatures.
I wish no more than this, O Lord.

Into your hands I commend my soul;
I offer it to you,
with all the love of my heart,
for I love you, Lord
and so need to give myself,
to surrender myself into your hands,
without reserve,
and with boundless confidence,
for you are my Father.

You might now take a scripture reading from the collection of
texts (chapter 16) or from the gospels (chapter 15). You could take
the same reading morning and evening and stay with it for a few
days. Do stay with it, let it fit in with your pattern of living, listen
to what it says to you. Explore its richness. There is always something new to be found.

Other chapters might prove useful here also, like the chapter on
praying with the Cross or the Risen Christ or maybe the section
on praying in silence. You could also take one of the prayers for
those around us and for our world (chapter 8) or you might like to
make up your own.

End with the *Our Father*, the pattern of all prayer.

Finally, take the prayer of Cardinal Newman at the close of the
day, and a prayer of Celtic Blessing:

May the Lord support us all the day long,
till the shades lengthen and the evening comes,
and the busy world is hushed,
and the fever of life is over,
and our work is done.
Then in his mercy
may he give us a safe lodging,
and a holy rest,
and peace at the last.

Amen.
Deep peace of the running wave to you.
Deep peace of the flowing air to you.
Deep peace of the quiet earth to you.
Deep peace of the shining stars to you.
Deep peace of the Son of Peace to you.'
(A Celtic Blessing).

We finish:
In the name of the Father and of the Son and of the Holy Spirit.
Amen

CHAPTER 11

Praying at Mass

The chant 'Mass is so boring' is a familiar one which young people in particular have adopted as their own. One of the problems is that they can be right. From the cradle to the grave Mass is part of the scene for most Irish people, and this is especially true of rural areas. It has a great social function and is one of the great gathering places. For many however it has become a performance. It is often the solo performance of the priest. This can be supplemented by guest attractions like choirs, readers, ministers of the eucharist. It is others who are involved, however. The main body of people sit there waiting for it all to happen.

Mass was and still can be something 'done' or 'given' by the priest. Slowly but surely, however, some parishes are involving more and more of the community who gather and this is how it should be. Maybe having music or readers or ministers of the eucharist does nothing for some people initially, but it does open possibilities. The readers can begin to introduce the readings, and they can begin to meet during the week and discuss them and reflect with the priest on a possible sermon. The ministers of the eucharist could prepare a post-communion reflection and might meet regularly to look at their role and at the meaning of the eucharist. They can be involved in bringing communion to the sick and in visiting the elderly. This provides a valuable support to the monthly call by the priest. The choir can work more and more to involve the whole congregation in the parts of the Mass, by using pieces with a refrain or by repeating hymns until they become familiar. If there is a parish council, they could put together the notices and read them out. A small group might also meet to prepare prayers of the faithful or to organise a procession with the gifts which might have special meaning for the community on different occasions throughout the year. All of these things involve people and are signs of life and of a community truly at worship.

Does all this sound too much? I can imagine any priest reading this raising his eyes to heaven! The whole thing becomes too much only if the priest is expected to organise and keep all this going. If he does this it won't have much long-term chance of success anyway, especially when he moves on. One of the things that has to happen with the Mass is that people have to start taking responsibility themselves. There is no need for the priest to be stuck in everything. He might be there on the fringes and he might get the thing going, but he does not have to carry the can for everything!

Maybe you are a member of a local youth club or voluntary organisation. This could even be a sporting or social organisation. It is the parish community who gather, and all individuals and groups in the parish are part of this community. Maybe your group, or a few of you, might see a place where you could help. It may be a long way to the presbytery door and you may not imagine yourself as ever being able to do something like this but, if you don't, who will? It's your church too! It needs to start small but if there are others like you things could really happen over a few years. It needs to happen.

You might feel that right now this cannot happen. It might be very difficult in your local situation for any number of reasons. Keep thinking about it, even if it has to be put on the long finger for the moment. Discuss it with others and you might be amazed at the response!

There are also some things you can do in the here and now which may help your participation in your parish Mass. In this you have some claiming to do. This is your parish and you are part of this congregation who gather. You are part of this Mass, this Eucharist and all that is said and done does concern you. Even from a seat at the back, participation is possible.

The Mass is the Sacrifice and the Sacrament of the Eucharist. This is the sacramental meal of the Church which follows the example and the instructions of Jesus. The word 'eucharist' comes from the thanksgiving of Jesus at the Last Supper and this, in turn, is linked back to the Hebrew idea of blessing and praise of God for all he has done. The *General Introduction to the Roman Missal* speaks of the Mass as the summit and heart of the Christian life. In it, we are all invited to share in the memorial of the life, death and resurrection of Jesus. It is the focal-point of the Church at the local and at the universal levels.

Before Mass

Arriving with a minute to go and keeping an eye on the watch throughout might be a popular pastime but it won't do much to help. Could you get there five or ten minutes beforehand and use that time to get yourself prepared, get yourself in the mood, come to quiet in yourself? You might draw your thoughts together:

How are things going for me?
What's on my mind?
How did last week go?
Is there anything in particular I want to pray for in this Mass?
Is there anyone I'd like to remember?
What have I to give thanks for?
What does Mass mean for me? What does this Mass mean?

Preparing the Readings

Is there anything that strikes you?
What is the main message?
How does it fit in with the way your life is at the moment?
What is the word of God saying to you about the world around you?

Preparing the readings is also something that you can do during the week. You might be able to get the leaflet or a missal which gives the readings from week to week. They can become part of your prayer so that by Saturday evening or Sunday morning they have become very familiar. You need not take all the readings but a short extract, something that seems to speak to you, is an excellent source of reflection for a day or for the week.

During Mass
When it comes to the Mass itself, some people are often worried because they get distracted, their mind wanders off at various stages. During the Mass it might be good to focus on some particular section or sections. Try to really concentrate on these, make the words and actions come alive. Make them your own and allow them to gel with your life at that particular time. You could try to concentrate on what a particular part of the Mass is trying to get across or on what the words mean.

At the beginning of Mass we try to prepare ourselves, to draw our thoughts to God and to examine our consciences. This is one obvious place. You could also take the Gloria and the Creed, two of the oldest texts in the Church, and really concentrate on them. The Gloria is a great hymn of praise and petition. The Creed draws together the heart of our faith in God the Father, Son and Holy Spirit. Sometimes outside of Mass you might take them and pray them. Read them, see what they are saying. They are so familiar that we can often just rattle them off without thinking. They are powerful pieces and could provide much for our times of prayer. They are acts of faith. How sincerely can we make them? They are statements of what the Church believes. Can we make them our own? The same might go for the 'Our Father', the prayer of Jesus. Take it line by line, see what it is saying.

Prayer of the Faithful
What about making the prayers of the faithful your own, adding in your own particular intentions, making them personal? Think of real needs and real situations in which people find themselves. Open up your life and your world to God.

Preparing the Gifts
During the Preparation of the Gifts, we can bring our own gifts and needs to the altar in preparation for the consecration. Sitting quietly, we hold our lives open before the Lord, giving thanks for all that is good, asking him to heal our pain or disappointment and to help us to make new beginnings where we have failed.

BEGINNING TO PRAY

The Liturgy of the Eucharist

During the Eucharistic Prayer there is a chance to be at one with the disciples and Jesus at the Last Supper. It's not just a remembering, it's not just calling to mind. Jesus is here. He is present in his Body and Blood and he wants us to share in them. It is happening as it happened at the Last Supper and on Calvary and as it has happened ever since when Christians gather to celebrate the eucharist.

Before Communion

Try to prepare yourself to receive the Body of Christ. Remember what Jesus giving his Body and Blood for us means or can mean. Jesus gives his Body to you and calls you in a special way to follow him. This is his promise of life for you now and into eternal life:

> I am the bread of life; he who comes to me shall not hunger, and he who believes in me shall never thirst. (John 6:35b)

> I am the living bread which came down from heaven; if any one eats of this bread, he will live forever; and the bread which I shall give for the life of the world is my flesh. (John 6:51)

After Communion

After communion, spend a few quiet moments in heart-talk with Jesus. There may not be need for words. Just sit with him, be quiet with him. Ask him to be with you in all that you do. Open your life to him. Ask for his peace. Sometimes you might like to use a prayer and you will find some on the leaflet in the church. You could also use one from the collection given at the end of this book, or from the chapter on 'Praying with the Risen Christ.'

After Mass

At the end of Mass you may again like to spend a few moments in quiet reflection. There will still be time for a chat with friends! Having a short time of quiet before and after Mass will make it so much more meaningful. For those of you into aerobics or circuit-training, think of it as a warm-up and a cool-down. It makes sense!

Visits to the church
At other times during the week, think of a visit to Christ present in the tabernacle. The Eucharist is reserved here and many people have found a time spent before the Eucharist a very special part of their prayer. It is the presence of Christ par excellence, the living presence of his life, death and resurrection. It is our bread of life.

CHAPTER 12

The Sacrament of Penance

In all sorts of different ways, there are problems with the Sacrament of Reconciliation, the Sacrament of Penance, Confession. Many people speak of finding the experience of going into a confession box, or even of sitting down in a confession room, quite difficult. Many question the meaning of it. Why do we have to confess? Why do we have to go to the priest. Why can't it be just between ourselves and God?

Yet many are convinced that this sacrament is of great value even if, in some ways, it has lost ground. It is a very old practice in the Church. The power of the forgiveness of sins goes back to the gospels and there is mention of confession in the letter of James and elsewhere. On a purely psychological note, the practice of sitting down with another and baring our souls can be a source of great healing and of feeling able to start over. Because it is a sacrament, we are taken far beyond the power of the purely psychological into something that is at the heart of our relationship with God. Sacraments are vital actions in the Church which bring us along the road of salvation. In this sacrament we admit that we fail, that there is a fragility to our lives, that we are capable of doing wrong and of causing harm and grief. We admit this, we point to different experiences we've had, we look for forgiveness, we promise to try to do better, and we receive a penance and absolution. These are the essential elements and the experience has a lot to recommend it. It is a humbling thing in a world that values strength of mind and presenting a calm, unruffled exterior to the world. It is also one of the ways God lets us experience his love and peace.

The sacrament is not essentially about sin. It is about forgiveness. Forgiveness is there, it is on offer. With God there is always the chance of beginning again. The Bible is the story of all these new beginnings. The Church always needs this possibility. God's forgiveness is limitless and never has strings attached. Once forgiven, the slate is wiped clean and God shows total forgetfulness about our sins. This is staggering in its implications.

The problem we often have is in believing in this forgiveness and in forgiving ourselves. God forgives and forgets, he holds nothing over. We will never be reminded, nothing will ever be thrown at us. All of us can be very good at dragging up old hurts and ancient skeletons, things that we think we have forgotten but which are often stored up in case they are needed. It is one thing to throw them at others; the saddest thing is when we use them against ourselves, as many people do. In Confession a lot of people include a little insurance policy at the end of their list: 'I ask forgiveness for all the sins of my past life, for anything I might have forgotten.' Sometimes they will bring up something that happened a long time ago and that they have confessed many times. God has forgiven them, but they haven't forgiven themselves. They're not sure; they confess again 'just in case'; no wonder the sacrament has problems!

There's a story about the Last Day. There is singing and dancing and celebration everywhere. All the suffering, all the difficulties, all the times of cross and darkness are forgotten. After a while, however, it is noticed that there is someone missing. Jesus cannot be found anywhere. He should be at the heart of the celebration! A group set off to find him and eventually he is found at the very edge of the crowd, staring out into space. He seems to be waiting for something or someone. They ask him what he is doing, why he doesn't come and join the festivities. He gives a sigh and says, 'I want to wait here, I'm waiting for Judas.'

God has this urgent, limitless, never-ending hope that we will all accept his love. It is not beyond anyone or any situation. Jesus lived out of love, he died out of love and he rose out of love.

Preparing for Confession

Many people come to the sacrament of reconciliation with the approach they learned in national school when they were first prepared for Confession by their teacher. Can you imagine a man or woman in their sixties confessing that they were disobedient? It happens! We get the familiar laundry list: telling lies, cursing, fighting, taking the name of the Lord in vain. For a child of six or seven these are things one might expect. One does not expect to hear the same litany at twenty or forty or eighty years of age!

We need to rescue the sacrament from this inability to leave behind the childhood lessons and the things we learned off. All that is needed is a bit of preparation and a bit of honesty. How are things going? How is life? Can we believe in this forgiving God, in this possibility of reconciling which clears the decks?

We need to look at ourselves, at our relationships with ourselves, with others and with God.

First of all ask yourself how things are really going:

What are the tensions and problems, the points of pressure?
Why do these things come about?
How do you regard yourself:
Are you your own worst critic?
Do you believe in yourself?
Do you despair?
Are there pressures from within or from situations at home, at work or in school which are leading to tensions and anger and bitterness?
Are their ways in which you are failing to love, to understand, to forgive?
What about those closest to me?
How do I show my love for them?
Are they the first to suffer when things go wrong?
How might I have sinned against them? (The same goes for colleagues or classmates).
How patient am I with others?
Do I always try to speak well of others?

Can I be envious or jealous?

Can I seek to use others for my own ends or pleasure?

How do I treat my friends?

What is the quality of my friendship?

How am I with drink?

Do I have control of it or does it control me?

What about sex?

Do I see it as a sign of love and giving or a selfish pursuit of my own pleasure?

Do I understand my responsibilities? Do I use pornography to heighten my own pleasure without thought to anyone else or of its meaning for my life?

In what way have I been selfish with my time and my energy?

Do I give thought to the less well-off or to the Third World?

Do I insist on getting my own way in all things?

Do I use other people's property with care?

Do I impose standards on others that I'm not prepared to live by myself?

Do I abuse responsibility?

Can I be trusted?

Am I loyal?

Am I just in my dealings with others?

Am I quick to judge?

Do I fail to give time to God?

Do I fail to respond to his love for me?

Do I turn to God in joy and in sorrow?

Do I give thanks to God?

Do I blame him when things go wrong?

Who is God for me?

In this as in all things we can only do our best. If we are to be honest in our attempts to look at how things are going, we will make a very worthwhile confession. It is a chance to take stock, to step back, to be honest and realistic, to look for forgiveness and to begin again. It is an opening up of our lives to God.

After Confession

After coming out, try to take some time to just sit in quietness, to settle in the realisation of the forgiveness of God and the act of confidence he is prepared to make in us again and again. Hopefully you will come to a joyful hope, a peace of mind and a new enthusiasm for living and for following Christ. This sacrament of reconciliation can be really life-giving and renewing. Hopefully, we will come to know its giftedness for our lives.

God the Father of mercies,
through the death and resurrection of his Son
has reconciled the world to himself
and sent the Holy Spirit among us
for the forgiveness of sins;
through the ministry of the Church
may God give you pardon and peace,
and I absolve you from your sins
in the name of the Father and of the Son,
and of the Holy Spirit.
Amen.

(Sacrament of Reconciliation, words of Absolution)

CHAPTER 13

Praying the Psalms

What are the Psalms?

Although some of the psalms are quite well known, our experience of them is often limited to coming across them in the Mass or on other liturgical occasions. They can suffer from being squeezed in between readings and may not be experienced in their own right. Modern music in Church has produced some beautiful settings which have become popular but again the danger is that we never really sit with the psalms and pray them.

Priests, religious and some lay people encounter the psalms in the Office they say daily, but even here the psalms may suffer from being part of something else.

We have a huge treasure in the psalms. They are essentially a record of relationship, of the ups and downs of life spent in relationship with God. They are poetry, heart talk, poems of praise and petition, poems commemorating history, poems recited on pilgrimage to the sanctuaries of God, poems used in the liturgy. They were written over at least five centuries and may originate with professional writers who composed them for the liturgy or for individuals. Their Hebrew title is 'Tehillim' which means 'praises'. The words 'Hallelujah' or 'Alleluia' are related to this word. Other words used for a psalm in the Old Testament point to a song accompanied by a musical instrument.

Most of the psalms fall into two groups – psalms of praise and psalms of supplication or of lament. They are heart talk and show great intensity of feeling. Nearly two thirds of the psalms fall into these groups. They can range from praising God for the beauty and majesty of creation, and from thanksgiving for help to the community or the individual, to pleas in the midst of illness, sin or threat from outside forces. Some of the psalms have powerful professions of faith and of innocence in the face of evil. We often find reference to enemies, to those who know little of the ways of God and who place the person who turns to God under huge pressures.

Sometimes too the enemies are the enemies of the world within and of the temptations of the world around us. In some of these psalms the cry is 'Why?' or 'O Lord, how long?' This has been heard from the human family always and these cries are heard throughout our world today. In the psalms, however, there is nearly always a note of trust, a conclusion that the Lord will respond and that the enemies of all kinds will be defeated.

The psalms are full of powerful and heart-tugging imagery. We find reference to beasts of prey, ready to pounce. We see too the water that comes to bring life and newness to dry and arid ground. There is a great simplicity and boldness in the language and this is one of their great attractions. The praise given or the pleas raised up are delivered with great power. We see the whole range of human feelings revealed in the face of a God who seems to hide his face at times. God emerges, however, as both Creator and Saviour. Just as God saved the Israelites of old, the prayer now is that he will once more save those who turn to him. To possess God in your heart is the great blessing – the loss of God is the worst possible thing.

In the world of the psalms, a sense of eternal life as we understand it had not emerged and death brings the life of shadow, of life without God, of emptiness and greyness. There is a huge concern in the psalms with death and life, with illness and dangers. All these bring the threat of death, of losing God. In the world of the time, things could also be very black and white and the psalms can sometimes shock us with this approach. All of this is intensely felt however and shows a world as it was, not as some might have liked it to be.

For us today the psalms can be a tremendous resource. So little has changed in the intensity of feelings and emotions, in the restlessness before God and human experience. So often too a psalm can lift us to a broader vision. We can move with the rhythm and with the intensity, we can take the images to heart and let them put shape on what is deepest within. In praying with them, we can even allow a psalm, which doesn't seem to be in touch with our mood at all, to put us in touch with someone who might be at one with this psalm in a very real way. In praying the psalms we join with so many others of our brothers and sisters; we pray with them and for them as they do for us.

Using the Psalms in prayer

As already suggested, you might take a psalm as part of your Morning or Evening Prayer. You could also take one psalm for your time of prayer, staying with it line by line, exploring it, letting it touch you. Even if it seems to say little to you in the state of mind you are in, it will speak of someone's experience somewhere and you thus join with them. It may raise you up and lift your spirits or it may lead to greater solidarity with those who suffer.

The following psalms are offered simply as a selection. There are 150 psalms in all. Find your own favourite ones, go to them again and again. They will nearly always have something for you like all good poetry and good prayer. Remember the stories of those who wrote them and those for whom they were written. Remember too all those who have prayed with them. Line by line they have a power all of their own which can carry you on eagle's wings.

Psalm 6

Lord, do not reprove me in your anger;
punish me not in your rage.
Have mercy on me, Lord, I have no strength;
Lord, heal me, my body is racked;
my soul is racked with pain.

But you, O Lord... how long?
Return, Lord, rescue my soul.
Save me in your merciful love;
for in death no one remembers you;
from the grave, who can give you praise?

I am exhausted with my groaning;
every night I drench my pillow with tears;
I bedew my bed with weeping.
My eye wastes away with grief;
I have grown old surrounded by my foes.

Leave me, all of you who do evil;
for the Lord has heard my weeping.
The Lord has heard my plea;
The Lord will accept my prayer.
All my foes will retire in confusion,
foiled and suddenly confounded.

This is a psalm of Penance, one of seven in the Psalter or Book of Psalms. It shows an individual crying out to God. It's a cry for help, a plea to God to intervene. We meet someone at the bottom, someone worn out, someone who cannot go on. 'I have no strength ... how long?' Save me in your merciful love'. There are times of exhaustion for all of us, exhaustion in the face of the burdens we carry, exhaustion brought on by our failures and our sense of deep personal failure. Is there any night when someone does not drench their pillow with tears somewhere? And yet there is hope. The psalm ends on a note of trust. The Lord hears, the Lord accepts the plea raised up, the Lord always will ... Because of this, all that weighs him down, all the old foes surrounding him will have to disappear like the ghosts of the night, thrown into disarray by the dawning light of God's presence.

Psalm 8

How great is your name, O Lord our God,
through all the earth!

Your majesty is praised above the heavens;
on the lips of children and of babes
you have found praise to foil your enemy,
to silence the foe and the rebel.

When I see the heavens, the work of your hands,
the moon and the stars which you arranged,
what is man that you should keep him in mind,
mortal man that you care for him?

Yet you have made him little less than a god;
with glory and honour you crowned him,
gave him power over the works of your hand,
put all things under his feet.

All of them, sheep and cattle,
yes, even the savage beasts,
birds of the air, and fish
that make their way through the waters.

How great is your name, O Lord our God,
through all the earth!

This psalm is a hymn of praise to a God who is Creator of all things and who has put man at the summit of that creation. God's majesty is praised everywhere and there are reminders of it everywhere. In all of this, however, God keeps man in mind ... God cares for the lilies of the field and the birds of the air but how much more is each human being worth to God! We are reminded too of our responsibility to the world God has placed in our charge. This is a psalm which was probably written for use in a community setting.

Psalm 16

Preserve me, God, I take refuge in you.
I say to the Lord, 'You are my God.
My happiness lies in you alone.'

He has put into my heart a marvellous love
for the faithful ones who dwell in his land.
Those who choose other gods increase their sorrows.
Never will I offer their offerings of blood.
Never will I take their name upon my lips.

O Lord, it is you who are my portion and cup;
it is you yourself who are my prize.
The lot marked out for me is my delight:
welcome indeed the heritage that falls to me!

I will bless the Lord who gives me counsel,
who even at night directs my heart.
I keep the Lord ever in my sight:
since he is at my right hand, I shall stand firm.

And so my heart rejoices, my soul is glad;
even my body shall rest in safety.
For you will not leave my soul among the dead,
nor let your beloved know decay.

You will show me the path of life,
the fullness of joy in your presence,
at your right hand happiness for ever.

This psalm of trust ponders our relationship with God and pours out a song of faith in a God who will lead us on the path of life. God is an active God who calls forth love and praise and trust. God's very nature calls for this response. Our experience of God is one which allows us to dare to hope and which calls for a full and lively response. Other gods offer nothing but sorrow. We fix our gaze on the God in whom is our happiness, our peace.

Psalm 23

The Lord is my shepherd;
there is nothing I shall want.
Fresh and green are the pastures
where he gives me repose.
Near restful waters he leads me,
to revive my drooping spirit.

He guides me along the right path;
he is true to his name.
If I should walk in the valley of darkness
no evil will I fear.
You are there with your crook and your staff;
with these you give me comfort.

You have prepared a banquet for me
in the sight of my foes.
My head you have anointed with oil;
my cup is overflowing.

Surely goodness and kindness shall follow me
all the days of my life.
In the Lord's own house shall I dwell
for ever and ever.

This is one of the most familiar and most loved texts in the Bible.
God is a shepherd and God is the host at a great banquet. These
are images very familiar to the world of the Bible. The Gospel of
John goes to great lengths to develop the idea of Christ as the
shepherd. A shepherd is known and trusted by his sheep, each of
whom is known to him. The shepherd watches over and guards
his sheep. At night he even lies across the gate of the sheephold.
Where the shepherd leads, the sheep have no fear in following.
There is nothing to fear once the shepherd is with them. God is the
holder of a great feast too, prepared for each one of us. He wel-
comes and honours each guest. We want for nothing. In the grace
of this care, this outpouring of love, what is there to fear? Our pilgrimage is to the house of the Lord. It is a blessed journey and one
followed in trust of God's goodness and kindness.

Psalm 30

I will praise you, Lord, you have rescued me
and have not let my enemies rejoice over me.

O Lord, I cried to you for help
and you, my God, have healed me.
O Lord, you have raised my soul from the dead,
restored me to life from those who sink into the grave.

Sing psalms to the Lord, you who have loved him,
give thanks to his holy name.
His anger lasts but a moment; his favour through life.
At night there are tears, but joy comes with dawn.

I said to myself in my good fortune:
'Nothing will ever disturb me.'
Your favour had set me on a mountain fastness,
then you hid your face and I was put to confusion.

To you, Lord, I cried,
to my God I made appeal:
'What profit would my death be, my going to the grave?
Can dust give you praise or proclaim your truth?'

The Lord listened and had pity.
The Lord came to my help.
For me you have changed my mourning into dancing,
you removed my sackcloth and girdled me with joy.
So my soul sings psalms to you unceasingly.
O Lord my God, I will thank you for ever.

This is a thanksgiving song. The person who sings it has faced the
nothingness of death, the embrace of the dust, and has cried out to
God. He has known the tears of the night, but he has come to
know the dawn too. For a time it had seemed that all was lost. We
have the powerful image of the person out on the mountain, alone
and dreading being lost at a time when it seems that God has hidden his face just as the mist hides the mountain. There are moments of confusion and great anguish; there are times when hope
disappears and the mist is down but there is always a call to trust,
to believe in the God who will hear the cry of the heart.

Psalm 42

Like the deer that yearns
for running streams,
so my soul is yearning
for you, my God.

My soul is thirsting for God,
the God of my life;
when can I enter and see
the face of God?

My tears have become my bread,
by night, by day,
as I hear it said all the day long:
'Where is your God?'

These things will I remember
as I pour out my soul:
how I would lead the rejoicing crowd
into the house of God,
amid cries of gladness and thanksgiving,
the throng wild with joy.

Why are you cast down, my soul,
why groan within me?
Hope in God; I will praise him still,
my saviour and my God.

My soul is cast down within me
as I think of you,
from the country of Jordan and Mount Hermon,
from the Hill of Mizar.

Deep is calling on deep,
in the roar of waters:
your torrents and all your waves
swept over me.

By day the Lord will send
his loving kindness;
by night I will sing to him,
praise the God of my life.

I will say to God my rock:
'Why have you forgotten me?
Why do I go mourning
oppressed by the foe?'

With cries that pierce me to the heart,
my enemies revile me,
saying to me all the day long:
'Where is your God?'

Why are you cast down, my soul,
why groan within me?
Hope in God: I will praise him still,
my saviour and my God.

In this psalm the writer places himself at the source of the river Jordan and he pours out a cry of yearning. This is a very beautiful and intensely felt psalm and has become a great favourite for many people. He is like the deer who longs for a favourite place, he thirsts for the essential, for what is truly life-giving. All around him are the temptations not to believe, to lose hope and his days are filled with tears. Has God forgotten him?

And yet he thinks of when he will join the crowd in the house of God and he makes an act of faith in the midst of all the despair. In the last few verses, we find more imagery that takes us into the mountain fastnesses and the depths of the oceans. These are places of mystery and power. These are also places where the Lord is to be found and where his loving kindness is made known. We are on the journey from doubt and despair to hope. Even in the midst of what seems to shut out all light, tiny glimmers of light wait to end the darkness.

Psalm 51

Have mercy on me, God, in your kindness.
In your compassion blot out my offence.
O wash me more and more from my guilt
and cleanse me from my sin.

My offences truly I know them;
my sin is always before me.
Against you, you alone, have I sinned.
What is evil in your sight I have done.

That you may be justified when you give sentence
and be without reproach when you judge,
O see, in guilt I was born,
a sinner was I conceived.

Indeed you love truth in the heart;
then in the secret of my heart teach me wisdom
O purify me, then I shall be clean;
O wash me, I shall be whiter than snow.

Make me hear rejoicing and gladness,
that the bones you have crushed may survive.
From my sins turn away your face
and blot out all my guilt.

A pure heart create for me, O God,
put a steadfast spirit within me.
Do not cast me away from your presence,
nor deprive me of your holy spirit.

Give me again the joy of your help;
with a spirit of fervour sustain me,
that I may teach transgressors your ways
and sinners may return to you.

This is the most famous of the penitential psalms in the Psalter. It is a prayer all the way from the heart, a prayer that recognises wrong-doing and is appalled by it. There is no attempt to hide, no attempt to find excuses. There is only the mercy of God. The writer catalogues all that has gone wrong. He knows what he has done and knows that ultimately he has acted against God. God can judge. He deserves his lot but he knows that God will bring him out of his sin and make with him a new beginning. The journey can be undertaken once more; he can set his face to the road in a new way. Through this new creation, through a pure heart, he can bring others on the road God has mapped out for him to follow. In our own moments of failure and despair, in the times when we know we have sinned, God is not going to crush us or add to the pain that can cripple. We must face the dark corners of our lives but we need not face them alone. There is One who will lead us out into the light once more. Like the pot on the wheel of the potter, God lovingly and patiently seeks to bring to life our own beauty and uniqueness.

Psalm 71

In you, O Lord, I take refuge;
let me never be put to shame.
In your justice rescue me, free me:
pay heed to me and save me.

Be a rock where I can take refuge,
a mighty stronghold to save me;
for you are my rock, my stronghold.
Free me from the hand of the wicked,
from the grip of the oppressor.

It is you, O Lord, who are my hope,
my trust, O Lord, since my youth.
On you I have leaned from my birth,
from my mother's womb you have been my help.
My hope has always been in you.

My fate has filled many with awe
but you are my strong refuge.
My lips are filled with your praise,
with your glory all the day long.
Do not reject me now that I am old;
when my strength fails do not forsake me.

For my enemies are speaking about me;
those who watch me take counsel together
saying: 'God has forsaken him; follow him,
seize him; there is no one to save him.'
O God, do not stay far off:
my God, make haste to help me!

But as for me, I will always hope
and praise you more and more.
My lips will tell of your justice
and day by day of your help
(though I can never tell it all).

I will declare the Lord's mighty deeds
proclaiming your justice, yours alone.

O God, you have taught me from my youth
and I proclaim your wonders still.

Now that I am old and grey-headed,
do not forsake me, God.
Let me tell of your power to all ages,
praise your strength and justice to the skies,
tell of you who have worked such wonders.
O God, who is like you?

You have burdened me with bitter troubles
but you will give me back my life.
You will raise me from the depths of the earth;
you will exalt me and console me again.

And all day long my tongue
shall tell the tale of your justice:
for they are put to shame and disgrace,
all those who seek to harm me.

We have here a prayer of a sick and burdened old man who, in the face of great troubles, thinks back to the way God has carried him in the past. He calls on God to be a rock for him, a place of safety to which he can anchor himself. From his youngest years God has been with him, God has done mighty things and now he needs God in his old age. Others might say that God has forsaken him but he will not. He has only hope and praise. No matter what comes his way, God will raise him up and he will never neglect to give thanks. Many people receive many burdens in life. Often it seems that the human spirit cannot but be crushed in the face of life. And yet some have faith – the ravages of the years deepen their faith and bring them a great peace which seems a contradiction! The cross and the resurrection move side by side through our lives.

Psalm 103
My soul, give thanks to the Lord,
all my being, bless his holy name.
My soul, give thanks to the Lord
and never forget all his blessings.

It is he who forgives all your guilt,
who heals every one of your ills,
who redeems your life from the grave,
who crowns you with love and compassion,
who fills your life with good things,
renewing your youth like an eagle's.

The Lord does deeds of justice,
gives judgment for all who are oppressed.
He made known his ways to Moses
and his deeds to Israel's sons.

The Lord is compassion and love,
slow to anger and rich in mercy.
His wrath will come to an end;
he will not be angry for ever.
He does not treat us according to our sins
nor repay us according to our faults.

For as the heavens are high above the earth
so strong is his love for those who fear him.
As far as the east is from the west
so far does he remove our sins.

As a father has compassion on his sons,
the Lord has pity on those who fear him;
for he knows of what we are made,
he remembers that we are dust.

As for man, his days are like grass;
he flowers like the flower of the field;
the wind blows and he is gone
and his place never sees him again.

But the love of the Lord is everlasting
upon those who hold him in fear;
his justice reaches out to children's children
when they keep his covenant in truth,
when they keep his will in their mind.

The Lord has set his sway in heaven
and his kingdom is ruling over all.
Give thanks to the Lord, all his angels,
mighty in power, fulfilling his word,
who heed the voice of his word.

Give thanks to the Lord, all his hosts,
his servants who do his will.
Give thanks to the Lord, all his works,
in every place where he rules.
My soul, gives thanks to the Lord!

Here we have a hymn of thanksgiving, a deeply felt prayer which rejoices in the mercy and goodness of God. Our God is a God of forgiveness and healing. Where we or others might rush to condemn, God is there already bringing healing and new life. 'He does not treat us according to our faults.' Someone has said that in facing a day of judgement he would much prefer to have God as a judge. He wouldn't trust anyone else to do it. The Lord 'knows of what we are made'. When everything else disappears there is only his everlasting love. This is our hope, this is our joy.

Psalm 139

O Lord, you search me and you know me,
you know my resting and my rising,
you discern my purpose from afar.
You mark when I walk or lie down,
all my ways lie open to you.

Before ever a word is on my tongue
you know it, O Lord, through and through.
Behind and before you besieged me,
your hand ever laid upon me.
Too wonderful for me, this knowledge,
too high, beyond my reach.

O where can I go from your spirit,
or where can I flee from your face?
If I climb the heavens, you are there.
If I lie in the grave, you are there.

If I take the wings of the dawn
and dwell at the sea's furthest end,
even darkness is not dark for you
and the night is as clear as the day.

For it was you who created my being,
knit me together in my mother's womb.
I thank you for the wonder of my being,
for the wonders of all your creation.

Already you knew my soul,
my body held no secret from you
when I was being fashioned in secret
and moulded in the depths of the earth.

O God, that you would slay the wicked!
Men of blood, keep far away from me!
with deceit they rebel against you
and set your designs at naught.

Do I not hate those who hate you,
abhor those who rise against you?
I hate them with a perfect hate
and they are foes to me.

O search me, God, and know my heart.
O test me and know my thoughts.
See that I follow not the wrong path
and lead me in the path of life eternal.

This too is a very famous psalm, often known as the 'Hound of Heaven'. The Old Testament has many gems of very personal and intense meetings between God and humanity. This is one of the most beautiful. Like the sun which never sets, God shines, he waits, he knows. Whatever we might say or do it has a place and God is waiting there before us. This is not to point to God as some sort of a brooding presence, waiting to catch us out, always one step ahead. God is the potter, watching over his creation, guiding and guarding. God invites, he opens up the possibilities, he holds us fast. He sees the wonder of our being even when we don't. God has not programmed our lives for us. We shouldn't be fatalistic. God has perfect knowledge and vision but, like a bird taking its young to the edge of the nest, God will only anxiously watch, encourage and invite. The writer feels powerfully about the wicked and urges a suitable end. This is in the mood of the time and points to the intensity of feeling of the writer.

Psalm 62

O God, you are my God, for you I long;
for you my soul is thirsting.
My body pines for you
like a dry, weary land without water.
So I gaze on you in the sanctuary
to see your strength and your glory.

For your love is better than life,
my lips will speak your praise.
So I will bless you all my life,
in your name I will lift up my hands.
My soul shall be filled as with a banquet,
my mouth shall praise you with joy.

On my bed I remember you.
On you I muse through the night
for you have been my help;
in the shadow of your wings I rejoice.
My soul clings to you;
your right hand holds me fast.

In this psalm the writer longs to be before God in the Temple, he is filled with thoughts and memories of other times when nearness to God sustained and carried him. He longs for God; his very being cries out to him. He is dry, arid in the desert, and he longs for what he knows can be. God's love is better than life itself. He longs to spend his life in praise of God. 'O let all who thirst come to the water ...'

CHAPTER 14

Praying the Gospels

Many people have turned to the Bible for comfort and direction. Many are overcome by this big book, this collection of books, and they wonder how they can even begin. Some start at page one and quickly give up. Others dip in here and there and are amazed and turned off by accounts of battles, of campaigns of hate and corruption, by lists of names and family relationships.

The Bible is not just a book. It is a series of books written at different times and in response to different stages of the pilgrimage of the peoples of the book. The Bible is not a record of history and geography. It is a story of longing and new beginnings, a record of relationship and of search for meaning. It is the inspired word of God which chronicles this relationship and God's plan of salvation.

The coming of Jesus brings the Biblical journey to its high point. For Christians, reading the Bible is always done in reference to this event. In this short resource for prayer, I suggest that one way of beginning to read the Bible is to start with Jesus in one of the gospel accounts. I've chosen Luke and have chosen a series of passages for reflection which might lay the foundations for a more long-term relationship with the Bible.

Luke wrote his account of the life, death and resurrection of Jesus in order to deepen familiarity with the story of Jesus. He addressed it to a person called Theophilus, who may have been an official Luke came across or who may have represented a community for whom Luke decided to write. It's an account which is especially close to those on the margins. It seeks to touch people, to bring them closer to Jesus, to point to all that Jesus has done and continues to do. It was written, possibly, for a community under

---

pressure both from problems within and persecution from out-side. In Jesus God has brought to fulfilment the promise of biblical history, the promise of redemption and salvation. The word 'to save' is used again and again, more often than in any other book of the Bible. This salvation is for all and is of special appeal to the outcast, the stranger, the poor, the sick and the sinner. God makes a fundamental option: in Jesus he has chosen to be with those in need and those on the fringes. It is here that the secret of Jesus' coming lies; it is here that the promise of the Bible is fulfilled. The whole Gospel is dominated by the resurrection and by what the resurrection means.

One other concern for Luke is the place of women in the ministry of Jesus. In the society of the time, they too were on the margins. Jesus shows a special sympathy for them and it is Mary who is portrayed as the true disciple. No woman opposes Jesus. They show a special openness to him. They are the first to witness to and to proclaim the resurrection.

Another emphasis in Luke is on the place of prayer in the life of Je-sus. We see Jesus praying before all the important events. We see the spirit of prayer and relationship with his Father run like a thread through the whole account.

(For a fuller introduction to Luke and for a commentary on the gospel you might look at *Luke* by Eugene la Verdiere, No. 5 in the New Testament Message Series from Veritas/Michael Glazier or *The Gospel of Luke* by Denis McBride from Dominican Publica-tions.)

The following passages from Luke are simply a selection. After taking them as part of your prayer, you might then like to take the complete gospel and read it over a period of time. It is one ac-count; it has its own flavour and emphasis. The gospels don't set out to be complete biographical accounts. Each of the four was written for a particular person or group in a particular situation. In time you may come to read each one over a year or a number of years until they become old friends, until the living Jesus they portray becomes the One who brings his life to you through them.

You may decide to take one of the following passages as part of your time of prayer and incorporate it into some other suggested way of praying. You can also take it on its own. Each passage should be taken slowly, line by line. Sometimes just one word or phrase from the passage might be enough to think and pray about. Sometimes a phrase or a question might gel with something that is going on right now for you. When this happens, stay with it. You may decide to take one passage and spend a whole week with it, reading it each day, focusing on different parts.

It helps too to imagine yourself as being there, as being part of the event. Take the part of different people in the passage or of an onlooker. How would you have reacted? What impressions would you have of Jesus or of the situation? What would Jesus have said to you? What is he saying now?

The Bible is the word of God. It is something alive and active. It has an energy and force of its own. It is as powerful today and as real today as it was when it was put together. It is the story of a search and a journey in which we too have a part.

Luke 1:26-38. The Annunciation.

Mary's call and her response. Her confusion, her fear. What could this mean? Her 'yes', her first act of witness.

In the sixth month the angel Gabriel was sent from God to a city of Galilee named Nazareth, to a virgin betrothed to a man whose name was Joseph, of the house of David; and the virgin's name was Mary. And he came to her and said, 'Hail, full of grace, the Lord is with you!' But she was greatly troubled at the saying, and considered in her mind what sort of greeting this might be. And the angel said to her, 'Do not be afraid, Mary, for you have found favour with God. And behold, you will conceive in your womb and bear a son, and you shall call his name Jesus. He will be great, and will be called the Son of the Most High; and the Lord God will give to him the throne of his father David, and he will reign over the house of Jacob for ever; and of his kingdom there will be no end.'

And Mary said to the angel, 'How can this be since I have no husband?' And the angel said to her, 'The Holy Spirit will come upon you, and the power of the Most High will overshadow you; therefore the child to be born will be called holy, the Son of God. And behold, your kinswoman Elizabeth in her old age has also conceived a son; and this is the sixth month with her who was called barren. For with God nothing will be impossible.' And Mary said, 'Behold, I am the handmaid of the Lord; let it be to me according to your word.' And the angel departed from her.

Luke 2: 1-20. The birth of Jesus. The first Visitors.

Jesus born of the line of King David; the link with the Old Testament and the journey in time and history to this point. Jesus born on the margins, visited by others on the margins. Who is this child?

In those days a decree went out from Caesar Augustus that all the world should be enrolled. This was the first enrollment, when Quirinius was governor of Syria. And all went to be enrolled, each to his own city. And Joseph also went up from Galilee, from the city of Nazareth, to Judea, to the city of David, which is called Bethlehem, because he was of the house and lineage of David, to be enrolled with Mary, his betrothed, who was with child. And while they were there, the time came for her to be delivered. And she gave birth to her first-born son and wrapped him in swaddling cloths, and laid him in a manger, because there was no place for them in the inn.

And in that region there were shepherds out in the field, keeping watch over their flock by night. And the angel of the Lord appeared to them, and the glory of the Lord shone around them, and they were filled with fear. And the angel said to them, 'Be not afraid; for behold, I bring you good news of a great joy which will come to all the people, for to you is born this day in the city of David a Saviour, who is Christ the Lord. And this will be a sign for you: you will find the babe wrapped in swaddling cloths and lying in a manger.' And suddenly there was with the angel a multitude of the heavenly host praising God and saying,

Glory to God in the highest, and on earth peace among men with whom he is pleased!

When the angels went away from them into heaven, the shepherds said to one another, 'Let us go over to Bethlehem and see this thing that has happened, which the Lord has made known to us.' And they went with haste, and found Mary and Joseph, and the babe lying in the manger. And when they saw it they made known the saying which had been told them concerning this child; and all who heard it wondered at what the shepherds told them. But Mary kept all these things, pondering them in her heart.

Luke 4: 16-21. Jesus comes to Nazareth. The Ministry begins.

A prophet in his own country. Who can this be? The fulfilment of the Scriptures. The programme for the ministry ahead.

And he came to Nazareth, where he had been brought up; and he went to the synagogue, as his custom was, on the sabbath day. And he stood up to read; and there was given to him the book of the prophet Isaiah. He opened the book and found the place where it was written:

'The Spirit of the Lord is upon me, because he has anointed me to preach good news to the poor. He has sent me to proclaim release to the captives and recovering of sight to the blind, to set at liberty those who are oppressed, to proclaim the acceptable year of the Lord.'

And he closed the book, and gave it back to the attendant, and sat down; and the eyes of all in the synagogue were fixed on him. And he began to say to them, 'Today this scripture has been fulfilled in your hearing.'

Luke 15: 4-7. God's option for the lost sheep.

This love that knows no bounds, that never excludes. The God who loves like this. The God who invites us to hope and to keep beginning.

'What man of you, having a hundred sheep, if he has lost one of them, does not leave the ninety-nine in the wilderness, and go after the one which is lost, until he finds it? And when he has found it, he lays it on his shoulders, rejoicing. And when he comes home, he calls together his friends and his neighbours, saying to them, 'Rejoice with me, for I have found my sheep which was lost.' Just so, I tell you, there will be more joy in heaven over one sinner who repents than over ninety-nine righteous persons who need no repentance.

Luke 5: 1-11. The calling of the first disciples.

Setting out into deep water. An act of faith. The unworthiness of those called. The promise of the call. Leaving everything.

While the people pressed upon him to hear the word of God, he was standing by the lake of Gennesaret. And he saw two boats by the lake; but the fishermen had gone out of them and were washing their nets. Getting into one of the boats, which was Simon's, he asked him to put out a little from the land. And he sat down and taught the people from the boat. And when he had ceased speaking, he said to Simon, 'Put out into the deep and let down your nets for a catch.' And Simon answered, 'Master, we toiled all night and took nothing! But at your word I will let down the nets.' And when they had done this, they enclosed a great shoal of fish; and as their nets were breaking, they beckoned to their partners in the other boat to come and help them. And they came and filled both the boats, so that they began to sink. But when Simon Peter saw it, he fell down at Jesus' knees, saying, 'Depart from me, for I am a sinful man, O Lord.' For he was astonished, and all that were with him, at the catch of fish which they had taken; and so also were James and John, sons of Zebedee, who were partners with Simon. And Jesus said to Simon, 'Do not be afraid; henceforth you will be catching men.' And when they had brought their boats to land, they left everything and followed him.

Luke 5: 17-26. The cure of the paralysed man.

Healing in mind and body. True healing. The forgiveness of sins. Who is this man? Acting through faith.

On one of those days, as he was teaching, there were Pharisees and teachers of the law sitting by, who had come from every village of Galilee and Judea and from Jerusalem; and the power of the Lord was with him to heal. And behold, men were bringing on a bed a man who was paralysed, and they sought to bring him in and lay him before Jesus; but finding no way to bring him in, because of the crowd, they went up on the roof and let him down with his bed through the tiles into the midst before Jesus. And when he saw their faith he said, 'Man, your sins are forgiven you.' And the scribes and the Pharisees began to question, saying, 'Who is this that speaks blasphemies? Who can forgive sins but God only?'

When Jesus perceived their questionings, he answered them, 'Why do you question in your hearts? Which is easier, to say, 'Your sins are forgiven you,' or to say, 'Rise and walk?' But that you may know that the Son of man has authority on earth to forgive sins,' – he said to the man who was paralysed – 'I say to you, rise, take up your bed and go home.' And immediately he rose before them, and took up that on which he lay, and went home, glorifying God.

Luke 6:27-35. Loving your enemies.

The values of the Kingdom of God. Who can say it will be easy? True love and its implications. The amount we measure out ...

'But I say to you that hear, love your enemies, do good to those who hate you, bless those who curse you, pray for those who abuse you. To him who strikes you on the cheek, offer the other also; and from him who takes away your cloak do not withold your coat as well. Give to every one who begs from you; and of him who takes away your goods do not ask them again. And as you wish that men would do to you, do so to them.

'If you love those who love you, what credit is that to you? For even sinners love those who love them. And if you do good to those who do good to you, what credit is that to you? For even sinners do the same. And if you lend to those from whom you hope to receive, what credit is that to you? Even sinners lend to sinners, to receive as much again.

But love your enemies, and do good, and lend, expecting nothing in return; and your reward will be great, and you will be sons of the Most High; for he is kind to the ungrateful and the selfish.

Luke 12:22-32. Daring to trust.

Why worry? Dare you believe in the Father's love? The fullness of that love. Being free to live the kingdom. The kingdom that is not earned.

And he said to his disciples, 'Therefore I tell you, do not be anxious about your life, what you shall eat, nor about your body, what you shall put on. For life is more than food, and the body more than clothing. Consider the ravens: they neither sow nor reap, they have neither storehouse nor barn, and yet God feeds them. Of how much more value are you than the birds! And which of you by being anxious can add a cubit to his span of life?' If then you are not able to do as small a thing as that, why are you anxious about the rest? Consider the lilies, how they grow; they neither toil nor spin; yet I tell you, even Solomon in all his glory was not arrayed like one of these. But if God so clothes the grass which is alive in the field today and tomorrow is thrown into the oven, how much more will he clothe you, O men of little faith? And do not seek what you are to eat and what you are to drink, nor be of anxious mind. For all the nations of the world seek these things; and your Father knows that you need them. Instead seek his kingdom, and these things shall be yours as well.

'Fear not, little flock, for it is your Father's good pleasure to give you the kingdom.

Luke 7:36-50. The woman who was a sinner.

Jesus among the Pharisees and sinners. The welcome he got. An act of sorrow, a moment of forgiveness, the response of the one forgiven. Peace be with you, it is I.

One of the Pharisees asked him to eat with him, and he went into the Pharisee's house, and sat at the table. And behold, a woman of the city, who was a sinner, when she learned that he was sitting at the table in the Pharisee's house, brought an alabaster flask of ointment, and standing behind him at his feet, weeping, she began to wet his feet with her tears, and wiped them with the hair of her head, and kissed his feet, and anointed them with the ointment.

Now when the Pharisee who had invited him saw it, he said to himself, 'If this man were a prophet, he would have known who and what sort of woman this is who is touching him, for she is a sinner.' And Jesus answering said to him, 'Simon, I have something to say to you.' And he answered, 'What is it, Teacher?' 'A certain creditor had two debtors; one owed five hundred denarii, and the other fifty. When they could not pay, he forgave them both. Now which of them will love him more?'

Simon answered, 'The one, I suppose, to whom he forgave more.' And he said to him, 'You have judged rightly.' Then turning toward the woman he said to Simon, 'Do you see this woman? I entered your house, you gave me no water for my feet, but she has wet my feet with her tears and wiped them with her hair. You gave me no kiss, but from the time I came in she has not ceased to kiss my feet. You did not anoint my head with oil, but she has anointed my feet with ointment. Therefore I tell you, her sins, which are many are forgiven, for she loved much; but he who is forgiven little, loves little.'

And he said to her, 'Your sins are forgiven.' Then those who were at table with him began to say among themselves, 'Who is this, who even forgives sins?' And he said to the woman, 'Your faith has saved you; go in peace.'

Luke 18: 9-14. The Pharisee and the tax-collector.

Who is really virtuous? The risk of beginning to pray. The demands of heart-prayer. The simplicity of daring to hope and daring to pray. The God who waits at the back of the church.

He also told the parable to some who trusted in themselves that they were righteous and despised others: 'Two men went up into the temple to pray, one a Pharisee and the other a tax collector. The Pharisee stood and prayed thus with himself, 'God, I thank thee that I am not like other men, extortioners, unjust, adulterers, or even like this tax collector. I fast twice a week, I give tithes of all that I get.' But the tax collector, standing far off, would not even lift his eyes to heaven, but beat his breast, saying, 'God, be merciful to me a sinner!' I tell you, this man went down to his house justified rather than the other; for every one who exalts himself will be humbled, but he who humbles himself will be exalted.'

Luke 22: 39-46. The Garden of Gethsemane.

A prayer in anguish. If it is your will ... let that will be done. Who understands? Who is willing to lay down his life?

And he came out, and went, as was his custom, to the Mount of Olives; and the disciples followed him. And when he came to the place he said to them, 'Pray that you may not enter into temptation.' And he withdrew from them about a stone's throw, and knelt down and prayed, 'Father, if thou art willing, remove this cup from me; nevertheless not my will, but thine, be done.'

And there appeared to him an angel from heaven, strengthening him. And being in an agony he prayed more earnestly; and his sweat became like great drops of blood falling down upon the ground. And when he rose from prayer, he came to the disciples and he said to them, 'Why do you sleep? Rise and pray that you may not enter into temptation.'

Luke 22: 14-20. The Last Supper.

The eucharist. The nearness of the kingdom. Jesus' death and the euchar-
ist. 'Do this in memory of me.' The covenant made by the body and blood.
Where two or three gather in my name ...

And when the hour came, he sat at table, and the apostles with
him. And he said to them, 'I have earnestly desired to eat this
passover with you before I suffer; for I tell you I shall not eat it before it is fulfilled in the kingdom of God.' And he took a cup, and
when he had given thanks he said, 'Take this, and divide it among
yourselves ; for I tell you that from now on I shall not drink of the
fruit of the vine until the kingdom of God comes.' And he took
bread, and when he had given thanks he broke it and gave it to
them, saying, 'This is my body which is given for you. Do this in
remembrance of me.' And likewise the cup after supper, saying,
'This cup which is poured out for you is the new covenant of my
blood.'

Luke 23: 33-46. The Crucifixion.

The Hour of Jesus. The reaction of the onlookers. The two thieves. Re-
member me in your kingdom. Forgive them. The darkness over the land.
What will happen now? Is this the end?

And when they came to the place which is called The Skull, there
they crucified him, and the criminals, one on the right and one on
the left. And Jesus said, 'Father, forgive them; for they know not
what they do.' And they cast lots to divide his garments. And the
people stood by, watching; but the rulers scoffed at him, saying,
'He saved others; let him save himself, if he is the Christ of God,
his Chosen One!' The soldiers also mocked him, coming up and
offering him vinegar, and saying, 'If you are the King of the Jews,
save yourself!' There was also an inscription over him, 'This is the
King of the Jews.'

One of the criminals who were hanged railed at him, saying, 'Are
you not the Christ? Save yourself and us!'

But the other rebuked him saying, 'Do you not fear God, since you are under the same sentence of condemnation? And we indeed justly; for we are receiving the due reward of our deeds; but this man has done nothing wrong.'

And he said, 'Jesus, remember me when you come in your kingly power.'

And he said to him, 'Truly, I say to you, today you will be with me in Paradise.'

It was now about the sixth hour, and there was darkness over the whole land until the ninth hour, while the sun's light failed; and the curtain of the temple was torn in two. Then Jesus, crying with a loud voice, said, 'Father, into thy hands I commit my spirit!' And having said this he breathed his last.

Luke 24: 1-8. The Resurrection.

The women from Galilee. Why look among the dead? He is risen. The fulfilment of the Scriptures. The darkness is banished. It is accomplished.

But on the first day of the week, at early dawn, they went to the tomb, taking the spices which they had prepared. And they found the stone rolled away from the tomb, but when they went in they did not find the body. While they were perplexed about this, behold two men stood by them in dazzling apparel; and as they were frightened and bowed their faces to the ground, the men said to them, 'Why do you seek the living among the dead? He is not here, but has risen. Remember how he told you, while he was still in Galilee, that the Son of man must be delivered into the hands of sinful men, and be crucified, and on the third day rise.' And they remembered his words.

CHAPTER 15

Bible Texts

In the section on reading the Gospels some pointers were given on beginning to read the Bible. In this section I have put together a collection of passages, mainly from the New Testament. These can serve as a resource for Morning and Evening Prayer or as a collection to delve into at other times of prayer. They might also be useful for prayer at a group meeting or as a piece with which to start a meeting or discussion.

Many of the passages come from Paul or from those associated with the missionary journeys and earliest Christian communities. In the past Paul has been seen by some as almost an embarrassment because of his supposed strictness and his reported views on certain issues such as slavery and the place of women in the community. While not denying that there can be difficulties, it would be a shame if Paul were to be taken out of context or if we were to fall into the trap of dismissing him. In the letters of Paul we see him baring his soul, we see his struggles and his regrets, and we see too an outpouring of faith and compassion. Paul wrote in response to certain situations in communities all over the eastern Mediterranean and beyond. We see a living church struggling to come to terms with following its vocation and striving to grow.

Many of the other passages, from other letters of the New Testament and from the Old Testament, are simply favourites of my own and passages that I have stumbled across in my own prayer.

In using them, I hope they will give you a flavour of the kingdom, of the call to each one of us and of the journey on which we are. Make them your own. They are a record of faith, hope and struggle. They are the inspired word of God and this gives them an ability to change us. They are an attempt to write about and to respond to the God who loves us, who never fails to love us and to call us on. Sometimes it is so difficult to accept this and live it out. Sometimes we can nearly burst with the joy and wonder of this love. In the early Church this was their experience. It is no different today. There are always those who are in solidarity with us, those who struggle, those who find moments of peace and joy. We join with them as we join with the people of Paul and the early Church.

As with the gospel texts, take these passages very slowly. Stay with a word or phrase if you wish. Place yourself in the position of the writer. What might have been his situation? What is at the heart of the piece? What is God saying through it? How does it fit in with your situation or that of those around you?

Pray it, make it your own.

The texts are from the Revised Standard Version unless otherwise stated.

1 Corinthians 12:31-13:3

But earnestly desire the higher gifts. And I will show you a still more excellent way.

If I speak in the tongues of men and of angels, but have not love, I am a noisy gong or a clanging cymbal. And if I have prophetic powers, and understand all mysteries and all knowledge, and if I have all faith, so as to remove mountains, but have not love, I am nothing. If I give away all I have, and if I deliver my body to be burned, but have not love, I gain nothing.

1 Corinthians 13:4-8

Love is patient and kind; love is not jealous or boastful; it is not arrogant or rude. Love does not insist on its own way; it is not irritable or resentful; it does not rejoice at wrong, but rejoices in the right. Love bears all things, believes all things, hopes all things, endures all things.

Love never ends.

Philippians 2:6-11

Have this mind among yourselves, which was in Christ Jesus, who, though he was in the form of God, did not count equality with God a thing to be grasped, but emptied himself, taking the form of a servant, being born in the likeness of men. And being found in human form he humbled himself and became obedient unto death, even death on a cross. Therefore God has highly exalted him and bestowed on him the name which is above every name, that at the name of Jesus every knee should bow, in heaven and on earth and under the earth, and every tongue confess that Jesus Christ is Lord, to the glory of God the Father.

Hebrews 5:7-9

In the days of his flesh, Jesus offered up prayers and supplications, with loud cries and tears, to him who was able to save him from death, and he was heard for his godly fear. Although he was a Son, he learned obedience through what he suffered; and being made perfect he became the source of eternal salvation.

Ephesians 1:3-10

Blessed be God the Father of our Lord Jesus Christ, who has blessed us in Christ with every spiritual blessing in the heavenly places, even as he chose us in him before the foundation of the world, that we should be holy and blameless before him. He destined us in love to be his sons through Jesus Christ, according to the purpose of his will, to the praise of his glorious grace which he freely bestowed on us in the Beloved. In him we have redemption through his blood, the forgiveness of our trespasses, according to the riches of his grace which he lavished upon us.

For he has made known to us in all wisdom and insight the mystery of his will, according to his purpose which he set forth in Christ as a plan for the fulness of time, to unite all things in him, things in heaven and things on earth.

Colossians 3:12-13

Put on then, as God's chosen ones, holy and beloved, compassion, kindness, lowliness, meekness, and patience, forbearing one another and, if one has a complaint against another, forgiving each other; as the Lord has forgiven you, so you also must forgive.

Isaiah 61:1-3

The Spirit of the Lord God is upon me, because the Lord has anointed me to bring good tidings to the afflicted; he has sent me to bind up the broken-hearted, to proclaim liberty to the captives, and the opening of the prison to those who are bound; to proclaim the year of the Lord's favour, and the day of vengeance of our God; to comfort all who mourn; to grant to those who mourn in Zion – to give them a garland instead of ashes, the oil of gladness instead of mourning, the mantle of praise instead of a faint spirit.

2 Corinthians 8:12

For if the readiness is there, it is acceptable according to what a man has, not according to what he has not.

Micah 6:8

And what does the Lord require of you but to do justice, and to love kindness, and to walk humbly with your God?

1 John 4:11-12

Beloved, if God so loved us, we also ought to love one another. No man has ever seen God; if we love one another, God abides in us and his love is perfected in us.

2 Corinthians 9:6-7,10

The point is this, he who sows sparingly will also reap sparingly, and he who sows bountifully will also reap bountifully. Each one must do as he has made up his mind, not reluctantly or under compulsion, for God loves a cheerful giver. He who supplies seed to the sower and bread for food will supply and multiply your resources and increase the harvest of your righteousness.

Deuteronomy 6:3-9

Hear, O Israel: The Lord our God is one Lord; and you shall love the Lord your God with all your heart, and with all your soul, and with all your might. And these words which I command you this day shall be upon your heart; and you shall teach them diligently to your children, and shall talk gently to your children, and shall talk of them when you sit in your house, and when you walk by the way, and when you lie down, and when you rise. And you shall bind them as a sign upon your hand, and they shall be as frontlets between your eyes. And you shall write them on the doorposts of your house and on your gates.

Isaiah 58:9-11

If you take away from the midst of you the yoke, the pointing of the finger, and speaking wickedness, if you pour yourself out for the hungry and satisfy the desire of the afflicted, then shall your light rise in the darkness and your gloom be as the noonday. And the Lord will guide you continually, and satisfy your desire with good things, and make your bones strong; and you shall be like a watered garden, like a spring of water, whose waters fail not.

1 Corinthians 1:22-25

For Jews demand signs and Greeks seek wisdom, but we preach Christ crucified, a stumbling block to Jews and folly to Gentiles, but to those who are called, both Jews and Greeks, Christ the power of God and the wisdom of God. For the foolishness of God is wiser than men, and the weakness of God is stronger than men.

Colossians 3:14-15,17

And above all these put on love, which binds everything together in perfect harmony. And let the peace of Christ rule in your hearts, to which indeed you were called in the one body and be thankful. And whatever you do, in word or deed, do everything in the name of the Lord Jesus, giving thanks to God the Father through him.

Revelation 3:20

Behold, I stand at the door and knock; if any one hears my voice and opens the door, I will come in to him and eat with him, and he with me.

Zephaniah 3:17-18

The Lord your God is in your midst, he will rejoice over you with gladness, he will renew you in his love; he will exult over you with loud singing as on a day of festival.

Romans 12:9-13

Let love be genuine; hate what is evil, hold fast to what is good; love one another with brotherly affection; outdo one another in showing honour. Never flag in zeal, be aglow with the Spirit, serve the Lord. Rejoice in your hope, be patient in tribulation, be constant in prayer. Contribute to the needs of the saints, practise hospitality.

Romans 12:14-16

Bless those who persecute you; bless and do not curse them. Rejoice with those who rejoice, weep with those who weep. Live in harmony with one another; do not be haughty, but associate with the lowly; never be conceited.

Ezekiel 34:11-12,16

For thus says the Lord God: Behold, I, I myself will search for my sheep, and will seek them out. As a shepherd seeks out his flock when some of his sheep have been scattered abroad, so will I seek out my sheep; and I will rescue them from all places where they have been scattered on a day of clouds and thick darkness. I will seek the lost, and I will bring back the strayed, and I will bind up the crippled, and I will strengthen the weak, and the fat and the strong I will watch over; I will feed them in justice.

Ephesians 4:1-17

I therefore, a prisoner for the Lord, beg you to lead a life worthy of the calling to which you have been called, with all lowliness and meekness, with patience, forbearing one another in love, eager to maintain the unity of the Spirit in the bond of peace. There is one body and one Spirit, just as you were called to the one hope that belongs to your call, one Lord, one faith, one baptism, one God and Father of us all, who is above all and through all and in all.

2 Corinthians 5:14-15

For the love of Christ controls us, because we are convinced that one has died for all; therefore all have died. And he died for all, that those who live might live no longer for themselves but for him who for their sake died and was raised.

Ephesians 6:18

Pray at all times in the Spirit, with all prayer and supplication. To that end keep alert with all perseverance, making supplication for all the saints.
(saints = the community of believers).

2 Corinthians 5:17-20

Therefore, if any one is in Christ, he is a new creation; the old has passed away, behold, the new has come. All this is from God, who through Christ reconciled us to himself and gave us the ministry of reconciliation; that is, God was in Christ reconciling the world to himself, not counting their trespasses against them, and entrusting to us the message of reconciliation. So we are ambassadors for Christ, God making his appeal through us. We beseech you on behalf of Christ, be reconciled to God. For our sake he made him to be sin who knew no sin, so that in him we might become the righteousness of God

1 Corinthians 1:26-31

For consider your call, brethren; not many of you were wise according to worldly standards, not many were powerful, not many were of noble birth; but God chose what is foolish in the world to shame the wise. God chose what is weak in the world to shame the strong. God chose what is low and despised in the world, even things that are not, to bring to nothing things that are, so that no human being might boast in the presence of God. He is the source of your life in Christ Jesus, whom God made our wisdom, our righteousness and sanctification and redemption; therefore, as it is written, 'Let him who boasts, boast of the Lord.'

2 Corinthians 4:7-11

But we have this treasure in earthen vessels, to show that the transcendent power belongs to God and not to us. We are afflicted in every way, but not crushed; perplexed, but not driven to despair; persecuted, but not forsaken; struck down, but not destroyed; always carrying in the body the death of Jesus, so that the life of Jesus may also be manifested in our bodies.

1 Peter 4:8-11

Above all hold unfailing your love for one another, since love covers a multitude of sins. Practice hospitality ungrudgingly to one another. As each has received a gift, employ it for one another, as good stewards of God's varied grace: whoever speaks, as one who utters oracles of God; whoever renders service, as one who renders it by the strength which God supplies, in order that in everything God may be glorified through Jesus Christ. To him belong glory and dominion for ever and ever. Amen.

Philippians 4:4-7

Rejoice in the Lord always; again I will say, Rejoice. Let all men know your forbearance. The Lord is at hand. Have no anxiety about anything, but in everything by prayer and supplication with thanksgiving let your requests be made known to God. And the peace of God, which passes all understanding, will keep your hearts and your minds in Christ Jesus.

Philippians 4:8

Finally, brethren, whatever is true, whatever is honourable, whatever is just, whatever is pure, whatever is lovely, whatever is gracious, if there is any excellence, if there is anything worthy of praise, think about these things.

Isaiah 52:7

How beautiful upon the mountains are the feet of him who brings good tidings, who publishes peace, who brings good tidings of good, who publishes salvation, who says to Zion, 'Your God reigns.'

Romans 8:26 (New Oxford Annotated Bible)

The Spirit helps us in our weakness; for we do not know how to pray as we ought, but the Spirit himself intercedes for us with sighs too deep for words. And he who searches the minds of men knows what is the mind of the Spirit.

Isaiah 53:4-5

Surely he has borne our griefs and carried our sorrows; yet we esteemed him striken, smitten by God, and afflicted. But he was wounded for our transgressions, he was bruised for our iniquities; upon him was the chastisement that made us whole, and with his stripes we are healed.

Joel 2:12-13

'Yet even now,' says the Lord, 'return to me with all your heart, with fasting, with weeping, and with mourning; and rend your hearts and not your garments.' Return to the Lord, your God, for he is gracious and merciful, slow to anger, and abounding in steadfast love, and repent of evil.

Isaiah 49:15

'Can a woman forget her sucking child, that she should have no compassion on the son of her womb? Even these may forget, yet I will not forget you.'

Ezekiel 36:25-28

I will sprinkle clean water upon you, and you shall be clean from all your uncleannesses, and from all your idols I will cleanse you. A new heart I will give you; and and a new spirit I will put within you; and I will take out of your flesh the heart of stone and give you a heart of flesh. And I will put my spirit within you, and cause you to walk in my statutes and be careful to observe my ordinances. You shall dwell in the land which I gave to your fathers; and you shall be my people, and I will be your God.

1 Samuel 16:7

For the Lord sees not as man sees; man looks on the outward appearance, but the Lord looks on the heart.

Jeremiah 17:7-8

'Blessed is the man who trusts in the Lord, whose trust is the Lord. He is like a tree planted by water, that sends out its roots by the stream, and does not fear when heat comes, for its leaves remain green, and is not anxious in the year of drought, for it does not cease to bear fruit.'

Galatians 3:27-28

For as many of you as were baptised into Christ have put on Christ. There is neither Jew nor Greek, there is neither slave nor free, there is neither male nor female; for you are all one in Christ Jesus.

James 5:13-16

Is anyone among you suffering? Let him pray. Is any cheerful? Let him sing praise. Is any among you sick? Let him call for the elders of the church and let them pray over him, anointing him with oil in the name of the Lord; and the prayer of faith will save the sick man, and the Lord will raise him up; and if he has committed sins, he will be forgiven. Therefore confess your sins to one another, and pray for one another, that you may be healed. The prayer of a righteous man has a great power in its effects.

1 Timothy 1:15-17

The saying is sure and worthy of full acceptance, that Christ Jesus came into the world to save sinners. And I am the foremost of sinners; but I received mercy for this reason, that in me, as the foremost, Jesus Christ might display his perfect patience for an example to those who were to believe in him for eternal life. To the king of ages, immortal, invisible, the only God, be honour and glory for ever and ever. Amen.

1 Timothy 4:12-16

Let no one despise your youth, but set the believers an example in speech and conduct, in love, in faith, in purity. Till I come, attend to the public reading of scripture, to preaching, to teaching. Do not neglect the gift you have, which was given you by prophetic utterance when the elders laid their hands upon you. Practise these duties, devote yourself to them, so that all may see your progress. Take heed to yourself and to your teaching; hold to that, for by so doing you will save both yourself and your hearers.

CHAPTER 16

Prayers from a praying Church

To end this book of prayer and ways of praying I offer a small collection of prayers taken from a variety of sources. Some of these
are well known, others are not so well-known but come from
familiar people in the life and tradition of the Church. They may
help you to put words on your prayer from time to time, provid-
ing a focus and a thought. You can fit one or two into Morning or
Night Prayer as I have done in the suggestions for those times of
prayer. The road is long and varied, sometimes it is painfully
slow. Sometimes too it seems that with each step forward we take
a step backwards. It helps to know that others have gone before
us, that others have had their moments of peace and union with
God and their moments of crushing burdens and darkness.

One or two of these prayers and thoughts might also put you in
touch with someone in the Church whom you would like to get to
know better. Like all sections in this book use it in whatever way
helps you. May those who have walked the way before us help us
on our own path and may the witness of their lives and prayer
bring us hope.

St Thomas More
Almighty God, take from me all vainglorious thoughts,
all desires for mine own praise, all envy, covetousness,
gluttony, sloth and lechery, all wrathful affections,
all desire for revenge, all delight in harm to others, all
pleasure in provoking them to wrath and anger, all
delight in upbraiding and insulting them in their
affliction and calamity. Give freely unto me, good Lord,
thy love and favour which my love for thee, be it ever
so great, could not receive except out of thine own great goodness.

St Thomas More

Give me, good Lord, a full faith and a fervent charity,
a love of you, good Lord, incomparable above the love of myself;
and that I love nothing to your displeasure
but everything in an order to you.
Take from me, good Lord, this lukewarm fashion,
or rather key-cold manner of meditation
and this dullness in praying to you.
And give me warmth, delight and life in thinking about you.
And give me your grace to long for your holy Sacraments
and specially to rejoice in the presence of your blessed Body,
sweet Saviour Christ, in the holy Sacrament of the Altar,
and duly to thank you for your gracious coming.

St Thomas More

Give me thy grace Lord:
to set the world at nought,
to set my mind fast upon thee,
and not to hang upon the blast of men's mouths.
To be content to be solitary.
Not to long for worldly company.
Little and little utterly to cast off the world,
and rid my mind of all the business thereof.
Not to long to hear of any worldly things.
But that the hearing of worldly phantasies
may be to me displeasant.
Gladly to be thinking of God.
Piteously to call for his help.
To lean upon the comfort of God.
Busily to labour to love him.
To know mine own violence and wretchedness.
To humble myself under the mighty hand of God.
To bewail my sins passed.
For the purging of them patiently to suffer adversity.
Gladly to bear my purgatory here.
To be joyful of tribulations.

Julian of Norwich
All shall be well,
and all things shall be well,
and all manner of things shall be well.

Julian of Norwich
I saw full surely that wherever our Lord appears,
peace reigns, and anger has no place.
For I saw no whit of anger in God.

Julian of Norwich
So it was that I learned that love was our Lord's meaning.
And I saw for certain, both here and elsewhere,
that before ever he made us, God loved us;
and that his love has never slackened, nor ever shall.
In this love all his works have been done,
and in this love our life is everlasting.
Our beginning was when we were made,
but the love in which he made us never had beginning.
In it we have our beginning.

Julian of Norwich
By whatever means he teaches us,
his will is that we perceive him wisely,
receive him joyfully,
and keep ourselves in him faithfully.

Julian of Norwich
God of your goodness give me yourself,
for you are enough for me.

Julian of Norwich
We are enfolded in the Father,
we are enfolded in the Son,
and we are enfolded in the Holy Spirit.
And the Father is enfolded in us, and the Son is enfolded in us,
and the Holy Spirit is enfolded in us.

Irish Blessing
Deep peace of the running wave to you.
Deep peace of the flowing air to you.
Deep peace of the quiet earth to you.
Deep peace of the shining stars to you.
Deep peace of the Son of Peace to you.

Micah 6:8
He has showed you O man what is good; and what does the Lord
require of you but to do justice, and to love kindness, and to walk
humbly with your God?

Book of Hours, 1514
God be in my head and in my understanding;
God be in mine eyes, and in my looking;
God be in my mouth, and in my speaking;
God be in my heart, and in my thinking;
God be at mine end, and at my departing.

Prayer of Saint Francis of Assisi
Lord, make me an instrument of your peace:
where there is hatred let me sow love,
where there is injury let me sow pardon,
where there is doubt let me sow faith,
where there is despair let me give hope,
where there is darkness let me give light,
where there is sadness let me give joy.
O Divine Master, grant that I may try
not to be comforted but to comfort,
not to be understood but to understand,
not to be loved but to love.
Because it is in giving that we receive,
it is in forgiving that we are forgiven,
and it is in dying that we are born to eternal life.

St Ignatius

O Lord Jesus Christ, take as your right, receive as my
gift, all my liberty, my memory, my understanding, my
will; all that I have, all that I am, all that I can be.
To you, O Lord, I restore it, all is yours, dispose of it
according to your will. Give me your love. Give me
your grace. It is enough for me.

St Ignatius

Teach us, good Lord, to serve you as you deserve;
to give and not to count the cost;
to fight and not to heed the wounds;
to toil and not to seek for rest;
to labour and to ask for no reward,
save that of knowing that we do your will;
through Christ our Lord.

St John Fisher

Jesus, grant me the grace to love you.
O blessed Jesu, make me love you entirely.
O blessed Jesu, let me deeply consider your love for me.
O blessed Jesu, give me the grace to thank you for your gifts.
Sweet Jesu, possess my heart, hold and keep it for yourself alone.

St Benedict

O gracious and holy Father,
you give us wisdom to perceive you,
intelligence to understand you,
diligence to seek you,
patience to wait for you,
eyes to behold you,
a heart to meditate upon you,
and a life to proclaim you;
through the power of the Spirit
of Jesus Christ our Lord.

St Thomas Cottam
O blessed Jesu, make me understand and remember
that whatsoever we gain, if we lose you, all is lost,
and whatsoever we lose, if we gain you, all is gained.

St Anselm
Enlighten our minds, O God, and purify our desires.
Correct our wanderings and pardon our defects,
so that by thy guidance we may be preserved
from making shipwreck of our faith,
be kept in a good conscience,
and at length be landed in the safe haven of eternal peace.
Through Jesus Christ our Lord. Amen.

from the Irish
Christ be near at either hand,
Christ behind, before me stand,
Christ with me where e'er I go,
Christ around, above, below.

Christ be in my heart and mind,
Christ within my soul enshrined,
Christ control my wayward heart;
Christ abide and ne'er depart.

Christ my life and only Way,
Christ my lantern night and day;
Christ be my unchanging friend,
Guide and Shepherd to the end.
tr. J. Fennelly

Prayer of Saint Richard of Chichester
Thanks be to thee, my Lord Jesus Christ, for all the benefits and
blessings which thou hast given to me, for all the pains and insults
which thou hast bourne for me, O most merciful Friend, Brother
and Redeemer. May I know thee more clearly, love thee more
dearly, and follow thee more nearly.

Pope Paul VI
Make us worthy, Lord,
to serve our fellow men throughout the world,
who live and die in poverty and hunger.
Give them by our hands
this day their daily bread,
and by our understanding love
give peace and joy.

Ignatius of Antioch
Faith is the beginning and love the end;
and the union of the two is God.